Willem de Rooij

Fong Leng Sportswear

Table of contents

The Impassioned No

Stéphanie Moisdon

In June 2015, Willem de Rooij's exhibition at Le Consortium, Dijon bore the title *The Impassioned No*: an anagram—a multiplied, disjointed phonetic material, a protocol of reversal and restitution that the artist has often employed in the past. From this first phrase we can make out, in its latent state, something of the operational procedures recurrent in De Rooij's work, of his processes of collaging and of collecting heterogeneous elements, summoning the very truth of language to the threshold of the exhibition.

In De Rooij's work, anagrams typify a very particular determination to make an essential concern of signifiers, form, and representation. He reveals a different function of the exhibition 'text,' and of the 'work''s language in the text. As the potential site of a manipulation that more or less blurs the boundaries, rendering them permeable or unstable, between what the work says and what the viewer wants to make it say, anagrammatic research founded on a theory of language also directly implicates an ethics of perception. As such, meaning for De Rooij is not so much the finality of discourse as its surface effect. Meaning is neither lost nor in need of being found, rather, it remains to be made. Because that which is repressed is not sense, and even less so is it hidden meaning; it is itself a sign, which is replaced by another sign, a language in another language, interlocking, diffracting, migrating.

And all the art, which is to say all the effort, all the mischief, all the skill of Willem de Rooij consists in producing a patently opaque sign—a sign that resists signification. While anagrammatic structure insists on the experience of the sign, the sign's identity is multiple for De Rooij. The sign is always a manifold being.

It may be that, early on in this historic moment of mutating forms of modernity and of tension between the opposing forces of subjectivity and standardization, Willem de Rooij has understood it is necessary to look beyond the subject, the object, and their combination, and to think with a plurality of modes, with what collection and technique offer as alternative inventive dispositions; with technical folding, *détournement*, and assembly; with implications and complications; with the contingency and the failures of production. At the risk of a complex aesthetic and intellectual adventure, at the price of a vertiginous position, De Rooij seeks to be the witness and the producer of silent forms, of unspeakable transfers.

Since his beginnings in the 1990s, Willem de Rooij's work has been engaged in the production of boundary objects that imply worlds, diverse factories, and relationships of exchange and conflict. His work alludes to the different states of production—material or conceptual, abstract or concrete—as well as to intermediary spaces of representation that renew the question of images, their usage, and their singularity.

Willem de Rooij belongs to a generation that experienced the end of a system (none is everlasting): the terminal phase of capitalism, its structural crisis. It is a generation that witnessed the ceaseless accumulation of capital goods and the exhaustion of old relationships of power and distribution. It is also a generation that drew lessons from these experiences, among them, a way to end the neo and post dialectic, to explore different possibilities for narration and appropriation, and to thereby discover how one creates more complex networks of information—networks in which condensed and contracted forms (a weaving, a bouquet of flowers, a photograph, a film) can take shape without allowing themselves to be deciphered, named, or governed by the single logic of causalities, references, and significations.

To borrow a phrase, "there is (a) One" [*Il y a de l'Un*] in Willem de Rooij's work. We may understand this as a "One-all-alone" [*Il y a de l'Un tout seul*] that refuses relationships, the dialectic of the subject.[1] The series of *Bouquets* begun in 2002 is literally grounded in this logic of differentiation and isolation. Each flower is the unique representative of a species that neither repeats itself nor finds unison. The three *Bouquets* presented at Le Consortium formed knots, structures made of these unbridled units.

But there is also and inevitably the 'Other,' the alterity constantly present since the very beginning, as with De Rooij's collaboration with Jeroen de Rijke (1970–2006) and in the majority of his installations, which involve other artists or artisans, works or artifacts from historical or anthropological sources, and temporary associations that generate interpretations on several levels.

Thus the gigantic installation conceived specifically for Le Consortium, consisting of fifty mannequins and a sportswear collection designed in the 1980s by the Chinese-Dutch couturier Fong Leng, alludes to these collective arrangements as well as to the undecidable status of each item, both autonomous and connected, where the history of techniques and of knowledge are juxtaposed, joining the premise of the representation of a human group, a family with no kin.

Fong Leng's designs have played a central role in Willem de Rooij's work since 2006,

1 Jacques Lacan, Séminaire XIX Ou Pire (Paris: AFI, 1971), p. 92.

as evidenced by his display of several haute couture garments from the 1970s at Galerie Chantal Crousel. The theatricality of the outfits, contrasting with the style of this more standardized production, is suffused with the paradoxical ideal of an ephemeral beauty and the changes at work in the globalized fashion industry. Between rarity and consumption, from couture to ready-to-wear, we can see an entire contemporary history of work, of labor, of value and authenticity, as well as the two apparent faces of a single market of bodies and objects, both unique and multiple.

From the 'One' to the 'Other,' there is neither relationship nor harmony, nor is there a program, but rather the self-evident fact of an original conflict, the impossibility of a symbolic, orderly, signifying articulation.

Small Phenomenology of the Tracksuit

Philipp Ekardt

Gear before gear

Here's a peculiarity about the tracksuit: its prime design ratio is to be taken off. It thereby shifts the game of 'dressing to undress' from the arena of erotics to the fields of sports and athleticism (or rather, the potential reconfiguration of erotics that it offers is a little more complicated). The tracksuit's first definition is utilitarian. This is also the reason for a certain proximity between this garment and classic worker's outfits, such as the overall worn at the work bench—to which attire, however, the tracksuit stands in a complicated relation.

Initially, the tracksuit was neither situated in the domain of the everyday wardrobe, let alone on an elevated stylistic level, nor in the realm of actual sportswear. Rather, tracksuits are 'gear before the gear'—gear to be left behind to reveal the athlete's actual performance outfit. They are warm-up apparel. The tracksuit thus exists in a strange corridor, as a garment of passage one might say, worn on the way to where athletic action unfolds, as one leaves the locker room for the track, the stadium, the field—or as one leaves the house, for that matter. In this sense, tracksuits are preparatory vestments whose primary function lies in keeping the wearer's body in a state that prevents energy loss (don't get cold before the competition) or to maintain said state in between installments of a competition (think decathlon). As a protective, flexible and insulating wrap, it suggests a certain level of comfort. Further, the tracksuit is the gear that one gets back into once sport is over. It's the apparel of what lies before and after.

Per definition, in a tracksuit one is never quite dressed for the actual occasion; its rationale is that as long as the going doesn't get going, one might as well dress with no stress. Although derived from the realm of sports, the tracksuit is thus as opposed to the concept of 'high performance' as a narrowly tailored shirt or suit jacket is antithetical to the bodily attitude of slouching. The athlete's competition gear is designed around the strength of the individual's toned, athletic physique, which it clearly displays and which it only covers where the body actually requires minimal protection. A formal suit, or an actual uniform for that matter, 'props up' the body in that it provides an aesthetically and sometimes even materially stabilizing shell, a formally reduced and regulated, or, by cut and fabric, even a concretely 'stiffened' wardrobe. In between lies the strange zone of the tracksuit that, if dislodged from its initial functional context in the realm of sport, may hide or eventually reveal a whole array of body types, in the most divergent states of having been exercised—a sort of banal medium layer of bodily adaptability, lacking all mystery and promise, unless fashionably and stylistically retooled in this or that direction.

Stylistic options

Think, for instance, of a neat and narrow cut of cuffs; a particularly figure-hugging shape of jacket; just the right tuck. Or consider the tracksuit's current return in the work of contemporary fashion designers, especially of a younger generation: Telfar (monochrome sportswear, the label's logo a strangely displaced echo of the insignia of Sergio Tacchini); Nasir Mazhar (survivalist, warrioresque, neo rave); Astrid Andersen (flamboyantly indulgent; extroverted color schemes that would have made Gianni Versace proud). Or recall iconic moments, such as Whitney Houston in 1991 performing *The Star Spangled Banner* at the Superbowl in a white tracksuit with the most voluminous, puffiest of sleeves, and a peculiar band of black and white checkered pattern running around one side, giving the impression of Formula One race car signage. In general, the tracksuit's stylistic options seem easiest to explore when split into its components: the jacket, or the pants. If actually worn as a complete outfit, the piece can come close to a onesie—a situation that can only be redeemed with a certain stylistic go-for-broke game, as in Missy Elliot pumping her garment to the shape and size of a Michelin Man. And then, there's the odd, and strangely direct solution picked by Fong Leng, who simply identified the tracksuit as the most basic possible version of ready-to-wear for a clientele that couldn't, or wouldn't afford her couture designs—the easiest of pathways for the aspirational fashion shopper.

Peculiarly, in particular the 'synthetic' tracksuit always retains a residual element of 'formality,' perhaps a slight reminder of a latent proximity to the realm of uniforms, rather than an effect of mere uniformity. As much is evident when looking at it side by side with sweat apparel, suited or not, cotton or terry. Synthetic tracksuits never reach the full ease that sweats can offer; they are ultimately barred from attaining the full sovereignty of the casual. While cotton sweat can play the full spectrum of 'just hanging out' to the actually very elevated codes of distinguished relaxation or sports, the synthetic tracksuit is ultimately confined to a clumsier regime. Perhaps this comes down to a difference in associations triggered by different textile materialities? The sweat's cotton somehow offering a less 'worked,' allegedly more 'natural' appeal than the more 'fabricated' fabric of the nylon tracksuit.

Abusive matching

No stranger sight—and not in an exciting, but in a rather off-putting way—than a couple that collapses the potential lateral aesthetic expansion of the tracksuit (a garment that's designed as much as for the individual as for a team) to an outfit for two, producing a freakishily non-dyadic dyad, a narcissism either so overperforming or so deficient that it actually projects the look of one onto the other. Whatever potential stylistic interest the tracksuit might offer is here programmed into a testament of 'matching outfits.' A guaranteed "no."

Sex and the vestimentary vulgate

Tracksuits carry the potential for sexual charge, although the outfit does not necessarily solicit this potential. There is, first, the quite simple aspect of its swift removability that has garnered the garment the nickname *Schnellfickerhose*—'fast fucker pants'—among German teenagers, alluding to the minimized time of undress before body-on-body-contact. Which, by the way, parallels certain aspects of the temporal economy structuring the tracksuit's use in its original domain of sports: easy to get out of, easy to get back in, engineered for comfort while waiting for and recovering, or moving on from the action. Thereby, peculiarly, defining that very action taking place in between—sport or sex—as exercise. A tracksuit, in this sense, is what is worn when the exercising and performing body is off duty. Beyond the pragmatic appreciation of the outfit (a *détournement*, so to speak, of the tracksuit's initial recoding of the potential to undress for the purpose of sport), there is also its direct visual appeal, depending on the tightness of the cut, to produce a quite graphic impression of genitalia (male—especially if no underwear is worn), breasts (female) and buttocks (both). In any case, the modeling produced is direct, and the textile that is internally sculpted by these organs and objects of desire leaves little to the imagination (proverbially and literally)—what you see is (nearly) what you get. This points to another of the tracksuit's main characteristics: its general straightforwardness, often the antithesis of refinement. Or, to put it differently: the tracksuit is firmly lodged in the realm of the vestimentary vulgate. (This should not be confused with calling this garment 'vulgar,' although there are certainly many examples of vulgar fashion performances connected to this piece of clothing—think Juicy Couture.)

By no means necessarily garish, tracksuit aesthetics seem, however, to be very difficult to reconcile with strategies that rely on sophistication. Tracksuits aren't understated either, in the way that minimalist reduction, or a reliance on nearly neutral basics (the white t-shirt, jeans) could be. The tracksuit's directness thus at least tangentially tends to touch the crude, and where it is most effectively and richly incorporated into fashion subcultures—in rave and hip hop—it is because of its peculiar ordinariness, to which is added that minute, if crucial extra of a shift into the para-sportive; like a four-on-the-floor beat that is basic, in a good sense, but still a tad flashy.

Tracky-love as sociological realism

One particularly instructive and telling example can be found in the way in which tracksuits are fetishistically appropriated in male gay subcultures.[1] As embodied, for instance, by the British so-called Scally Lads, and facilitated by dating portals such as the appropriately titled *trackies.com*, the tracksuit here blossoms into a genuine apparel fetish. Interestingly, this fetish is not tied to a specific materiality of the textile (as is the case, for instance, for enthusiasts of lycra); nor does it center around a specific brand (although brands, and their knock-offs seem to be crucially important), a specific cut (say, short Adidas tennis shorts), or a specific athletic discipline (biking, speedos...). Rather, it is the tracksuit's perceived association with

1 In general, tracksuits are of course designed for all genders, and their harnessing for the purposes of sex is open to all sorts of sexual persuasions. However, there seems to be a particularly pronounced elaboration of such matters in one particular subset of male homosexuals, to which the following paragraphs are dedicated.

a mutual inflection of class and gender performance incorporated by way of the garment. These are, little surprise here, a roughish ideal of 'masculinity' that is constructed in conjunction with what is perceived to be 'lower' social status and a proximity to the existence of social pariahs of little to no economic means.

This tracky-ism is different from, say, the classic and certainly also difficult eroticization of an alleged 'lower' social position in the 1950s, like the sexing up of the wifebeater (think Brando), with its fantasies about handymen, auto mechanics, and so on. The preference for tracksuits also differs from, say, an aesthetic or stylistic, as well as an erotic, appreciation of work(er's) wear. The 'tracky' fetishist is probably less interested in a concept of a traditional working class, and more interested in a position of the working poor, or those who have completely fallen through the social fabric into a life between welfare and poverty-related crime. Although the tracky's erotic radar is problematically tuned in to what it considers a distinctly 'non-feminine' ideal of masculinity, roughness, or even violence at the alleged 'lower end' of society, he is sociologically speaking a realist: he does not desire the worker and his apparel, because that worker, with his intact class identity, and possibly even pride, is gone. In other words, calling a tracksuit—as some have done—'prole' is not just impolite and discriminatory, it is wrong, because all signs point to the fact that the proletariat, who would suit up in overalls at the factory, has disappeared. Yet somehow the tracksuit also speaks to this: not the worker's uniform, or the professional athlete's garment, it is now the item in which one hangs, stands on the corner, crouches, etc.—all positions in which time passes, and the activity on the horizon might be a visit to the gym, rather than 'work' in the classic sense.

Difference, Diversity, and Negation

Manfred Hermes

Willem de Rooij likes to keep things simple. A bunch of cut flowers, a length of fabric attached to a stretcher, or some 1980s shell suits can become the basis of a piece. A vase with dozens of flowers always makes for a lush, ravishing presence, but it looks particularly luxurious in the empty whiteness of an art space. What it does not stand for is a high production budget. And while the pictorial rendition of a floral arrangement is called a still life, 'saying it with flowers' gets a whole new meaning when the full range of variables is utilized for signification (color, fragrance, quantity, dimension, availability, provenance, type). De Rooij's choice of flowers reflects 'diversity' and implicates or metaphorizes social relations.

Similar to these *Bouquets*, De Rooij has had individual panels of material made to order and by hand. Creating the fabric from scratch, from the structural basis of the warp and woof, he combined filaments with diverging properties (width, structure, color, surface etc.) and derived metaphorical meaning from slightly differing weaves. The results vary slightly in regard to structure and coloring. Tugging them around stretchers, De Rooij converted the bespoke fabrics into reluctantly polychromatic monochromes (or knockoffs of the modernist monochrome).

As for the signifying capabilities of textiles, De Rooij added fashion examples. Fong Leng's designs became a steady reference because of the designer's Dutch-Chinese background and the aesthetic repercussions of a 'multicultural' reality and subjectivity in the Netherlands in the 1970s. De Rooij has taken a particular interest in her diffused historical styles and the luxurious use of 'ethnic' ornamentation in her pieces, enabling him to transform his fashion fascination into a post-colonial reading.[1] Fong Leng herself transitioned from couture to mass-produced streetwear in the early 1980s, participating in a growing interest in self-improvement regimes and in fashion's then-ubiquitous turn to the 'street.' De Rooij began to collect these suits, finding most of them on the second hand market. Though they were more restrained on ornamentation, Fong Leng had not totally abandoned 'ethnic' elements. She adorned some of the tracksuits with inlaid prints of a similarly syncretic appeal (via, for example, African, East European or Chinese influences). De Rooij has exhibited these suits despite their lack of material value and in favor of their somewhat pedestrian glamour; in addition, their bold asymmetrical patterns, saggy shapes and a color scheme bordering on the drab resonate well with current aesthetic sensibilities.

A museum can provide an attractive stage even for banal items, such as a pile of 1980s shell suits, and provide for their ultimate survival. To relate a piece of clothing to a sculpture or perceive it in architectural terms is not an uncommon analogy, just as it is hardly a new observation to point to the similarities of flagship store aesthetics and the art showroom. De Rooij's cool, dry, ultimately elegant presentation modes function accordingly. Boxes, boxy plinths or bases also serve as rationalizing and distancing tools, aimed at framing the visually pleasant, while effortlessly adopting, and possibly mocking, institutional standards of object display, enabling the most inconspicuous objects to yield visual pleasure.

For De Rooij, textiles themselves can be narrative devices. For his shows *Entitled* (MMK, Frankfurt am Main, 2016) and *The Impassioned No* (Le Consortium, Dijon, 2015) he dressed a dozen black figurines in Fong Leng shell suits, sorted by color. The mannequins insert a more representational aspect into De Rooij's social claims. He groups the (gendered) dummies in *mises en scène* that imply gender relations, the grids of desire, intimate couplings, chance meetings, all types of social interaction—or inaction, as some of these groupings have the alluring unspecificity associated with a fashion spread in a magazine.[2] The blackness of the mannequins seems to hint at the issue of race, but De Rooij asserted they were only chosen for reflectivity. The light reflections on their glossy surfaces are indeed quite potent, but with individual features erased and an emphasis on the silhouette, the figurines are mere abstractions or rather negations of the human body, their sleek black heads quite literally are like a void.

The title *The Imapssioned No* leaves one guessing as to what the "no" relates to. Does it indicate an opposition to art, to cultural or institutional assertions? Its modes of representation? Western concepts of fashion or history? Does it oppose worn out concepts of the art object, of authorship and subjectivity? Or all of the above?

De Rooij proposed a possible answer with another title, *Intolerance* (Neue Nationalgalerie, Berlin, 2010). For this museum exhibition he

1 For a brief account of Fong Leng's iconography, I refer to Andrea Viliani's essay "Luipaard," in: *Jeroen de Rijke/ Willem de Rooij*, exhibition catalogue Museo d'Arte Moderna di Bologna and K21 Düsseldorf (Cologne: Snoeck, 2008), pp. 207–210.

2 Some metaphors for social relations, like a weave for the 'social fabric' or a bunch of flowers for 'diversity' could be considered toxic: bunch in 'bunch of flowers' subsumes difference or diversity under an idea of unity and generality.

juxtaposed Hawaiian garments for sacral use and paintings by Melchior d'Hondecoeter (1639–1695), a Dutch specialist in bird depiction. Juggling the ethnological and the ornithological, the show's proposition backed a critique of (exoticizing) ethnological assumptions and, more generally, of 'art,' 'painting,' and 'museum.'

The comparative mode also suggested actual similarities. D'Hondecoeter's paintings, casual groupings of domestic birds, even poultry, with flamboyant tropical conspecifics in landscapes, may be easy on a European eye and produce placid feelings. On the other hand, an ancient Hawaiian cape with broad ornaments pixelated from millions of bright bird feathers may look breathtaking but very alien. Depending on perspective or knowledge, an initial assessment may shift. For instance, both productions may have required international coordination and division of labor. They can relate to purposes und realities now unimportant and unknowable. In much the same way both items can be praised indifferently for rarity, value, inaccessibility, beauty, or any other aesthetical stimulant. Or they can become an object of historical or materialistic research.

The Age of Discovery laid the groundwork for imperialistic expansion and the furthering of international trade, as well as for ethnographical research. As a major beneficiary, the Netherlands saw exponential growth of cities, immigration, financial markets and personal wealth, and the boom of the art market was a direct consequence. Paintings became sought-after commodities and status symbols for the nouveau riche and a bourgeois clientele.

In terms of a materialist argument, even a grand Dutch painting from the Golden Age can transform into something sober and pragmatic, or become as alien as an ethnographical artifact. In his show *Intolerance*, De Rooij underlined the possible slightness of difference by putting the exhibits in physical proximity. And yet the overall impression of the Berlin show was not quite unaesthetic; mounted onto a big white box of a wall, the garments and paintings looked rather stunning.[3]

De Rooij's productions are the result of curatorial efforts, and they have an essayistic side to them. They stick to a set of rules without being conceptual. Often the word 'concept' asserts pompous ideas of methodical control and philosophical entitlement. In contrast to this, an essayistic approach is able to operate more freely and may allow itself to move around the margins of knowledge. It seems to require an aesthetic environment that constitutes itself through collaboration, arbitrary connection, and research effort.

De Rooij renders his non-fictional narrations by way of object relations, images and words. Not every juxtaposition bears the specifics of a collage. His work relies on inventories, on lists, on borrowed things for temporary use. An integration of layers and heterogeneous motifs is unnecessary. These elements don't have to merge or build on one another. This is what I consider to be essayistic—the essayist does not need the thrust of 'theory' for legitimization. Adorno emphasized "the essay as speculation on specific, culturally pre-formed objects," without taking advantage of them only "to exemplify universal categories."[4] He went on to refer to Georg Lukács, who pointed to the essay's profound dependence on the historical and the past.

3 And this was quite literally a matter of lighting, and yet another example of De Rooij's competence for effortlessly adapting museum standards of object presentation: precisely shaped beams gave d'Hondecoeter's paintings an unreal diaphanous quality, they seemed backlit.

4 Theodor W. Adorno, "The Essay as Form," in: *Notes to Literature*, vol 1, ed. Rolf Tiedemann, transl. Shierry Weber-Nicholson (New York: Columbia University Press, 1991), p. 3.

The latter point resonates strongly with De Rooij's work. Within the historical mode, he follows diverging paths, concerning opposition, contradiction and difference. A spray of flowers, handmade fabrics, sacral capes or groups of mannequins in shell suits can indicate a slight difference or a hierarchy. In the show *The Point of Departure* (Galerie Buchholz, Cologne 2002), the duo De Rijke/ De Rooij focused on ancient oriental carpets, their ornamentation and its coding. A black and white reproduction of a rug was placed next to a black monochromatic photo, thus matching diverging approaches to abstraction and visual reduction.[5]

But Islamic and modernist iconoclasm did not stand on an equal footing. There was clearly a bias towards the non-Western, the 'ancient' or primordial, where 'departures' can occur. This was yet another link to an ambivalent negativist tradition in early modernism, which could turn this way or that. In Willem de Rooij's double articulations, difference sometimes leads to generality, and then to more difference.

5 The black photograph is in fact a print of a blank film still—its abyss therefore based on erasing filmic faculties like movement, light, image and narration.

Installation views

The Impassioned No
20 June – 27 September 2015
Le Consortium, Dijon

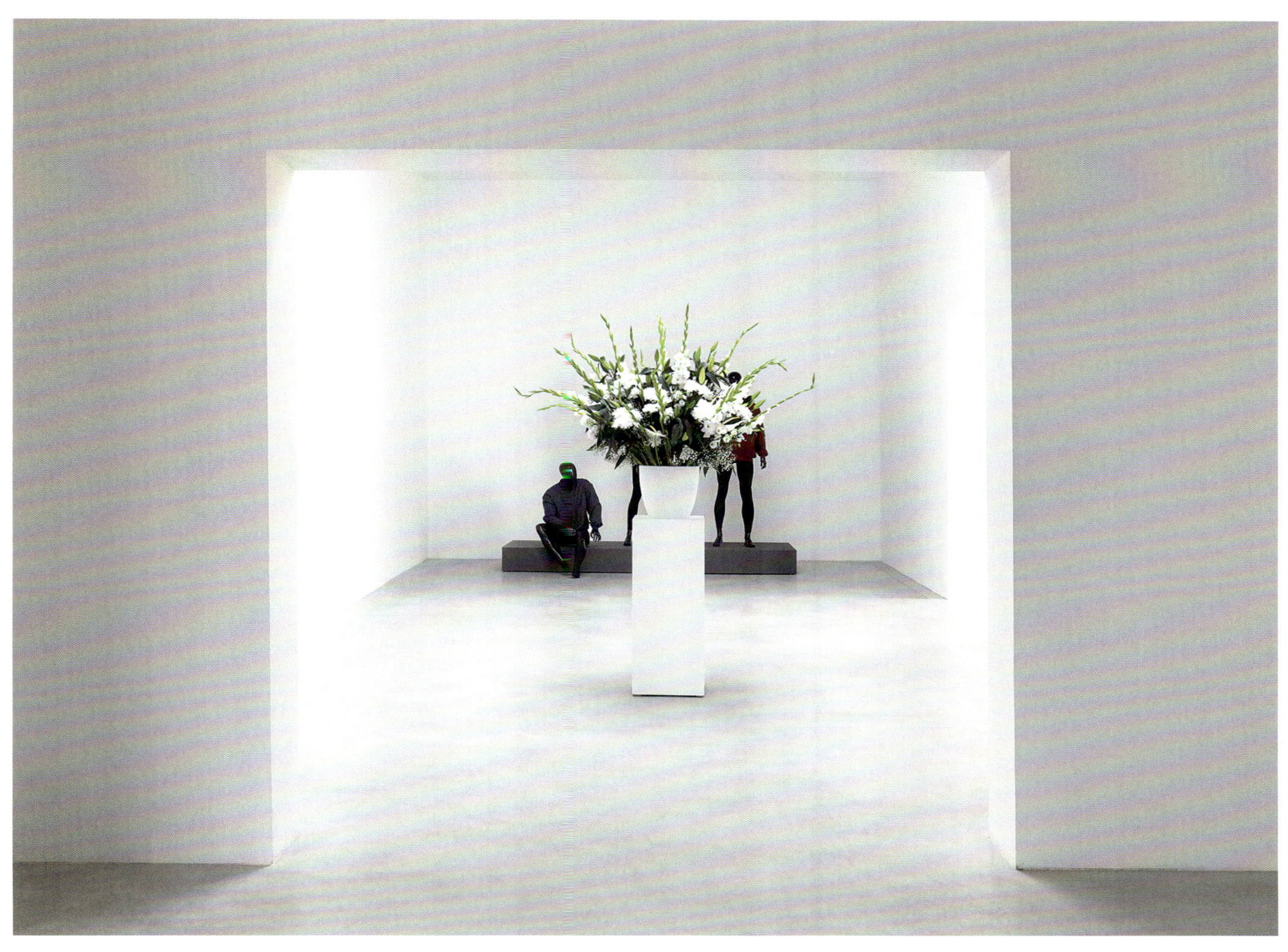

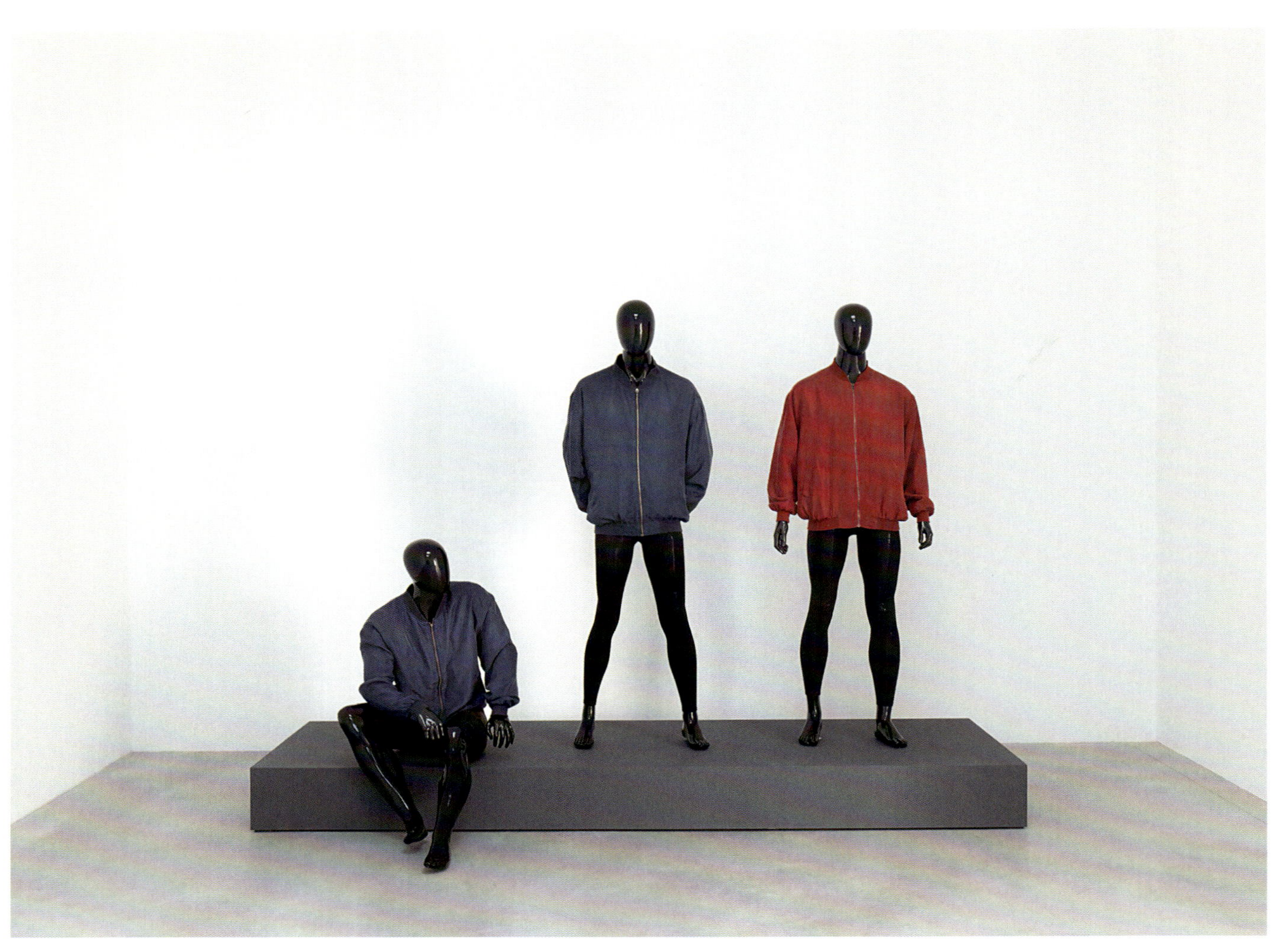

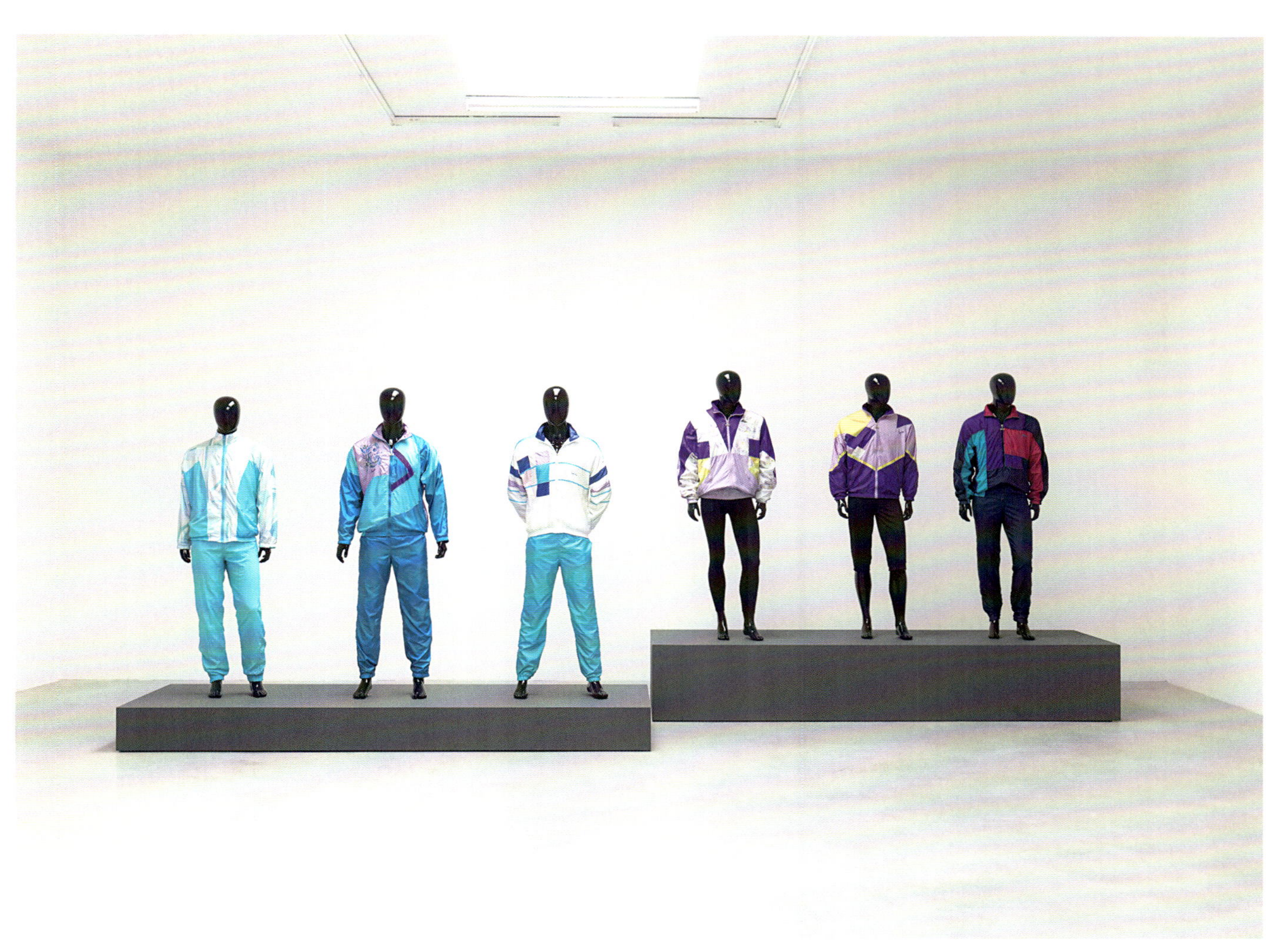

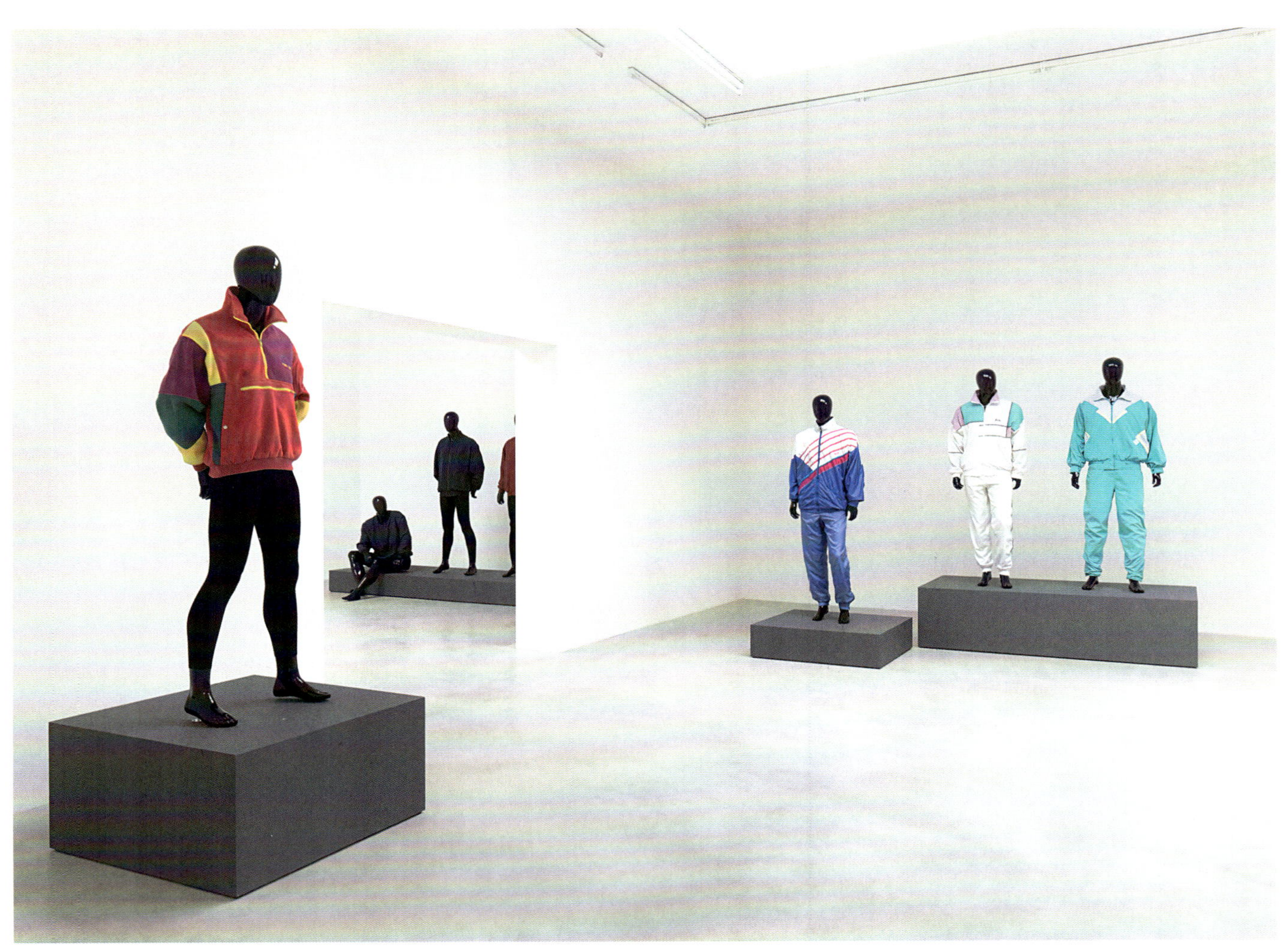

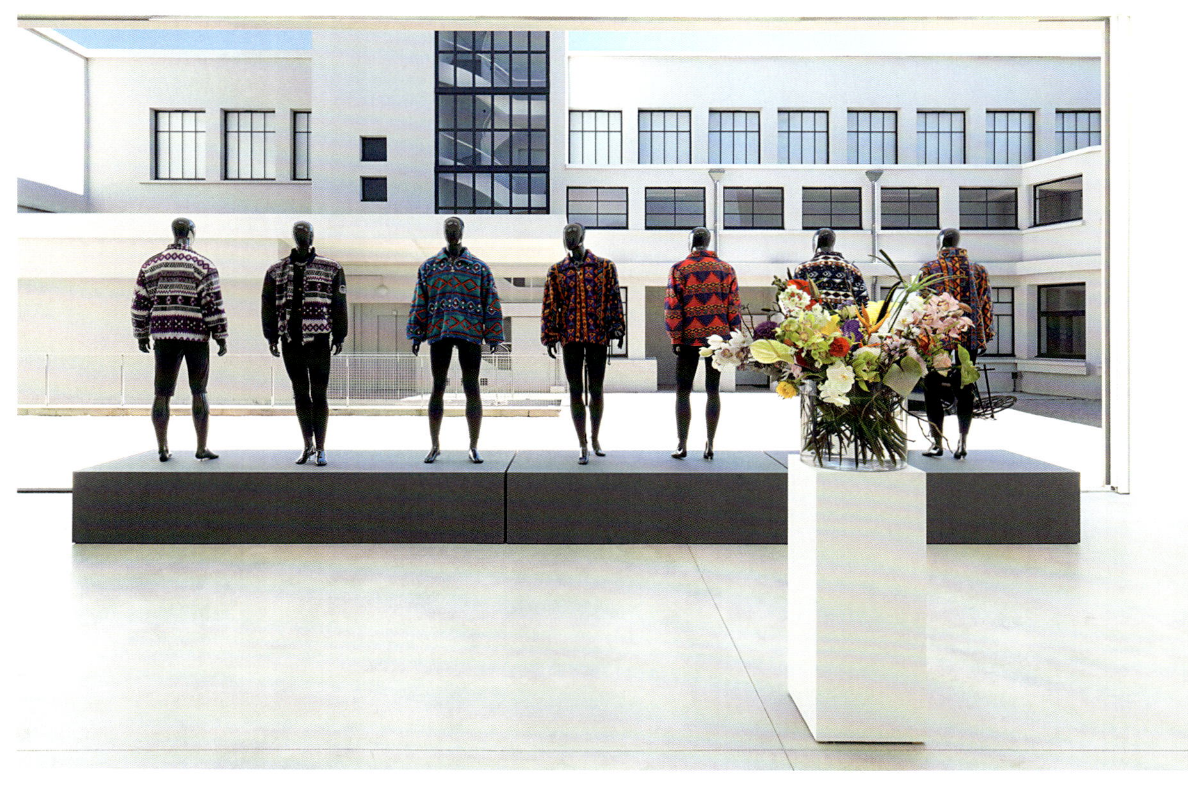

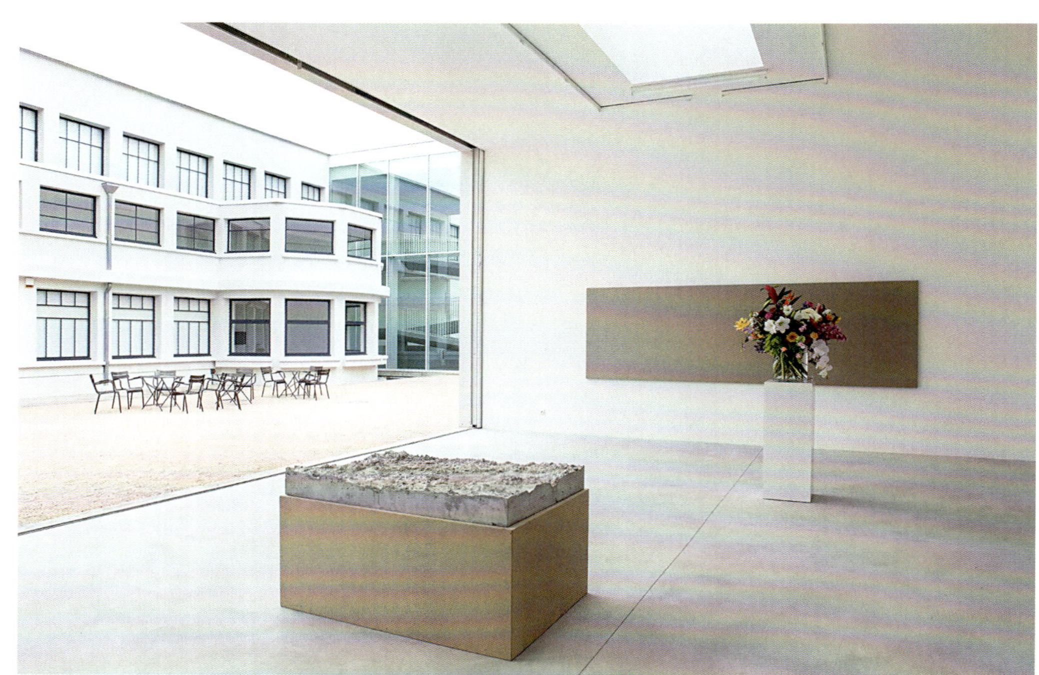

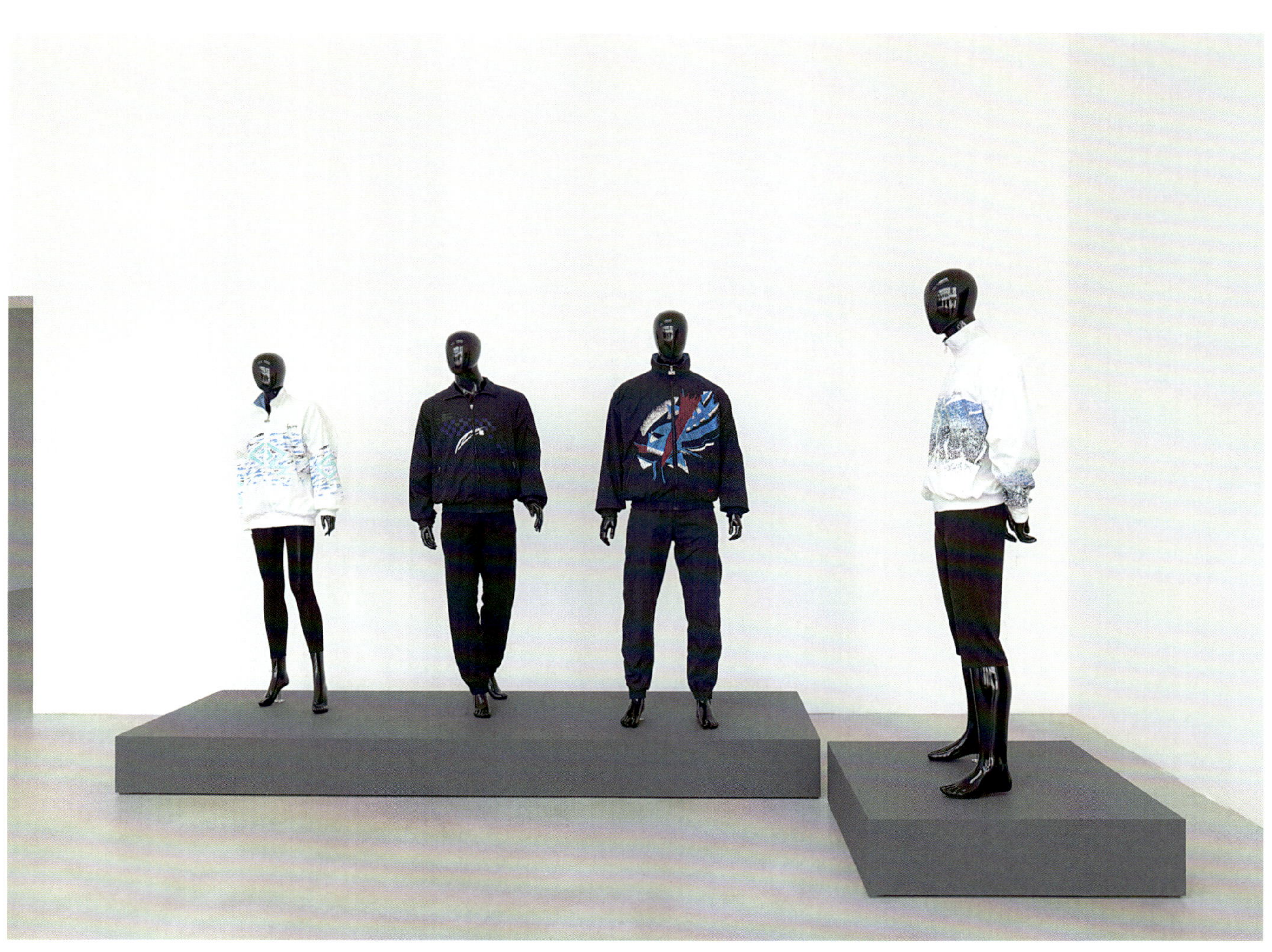

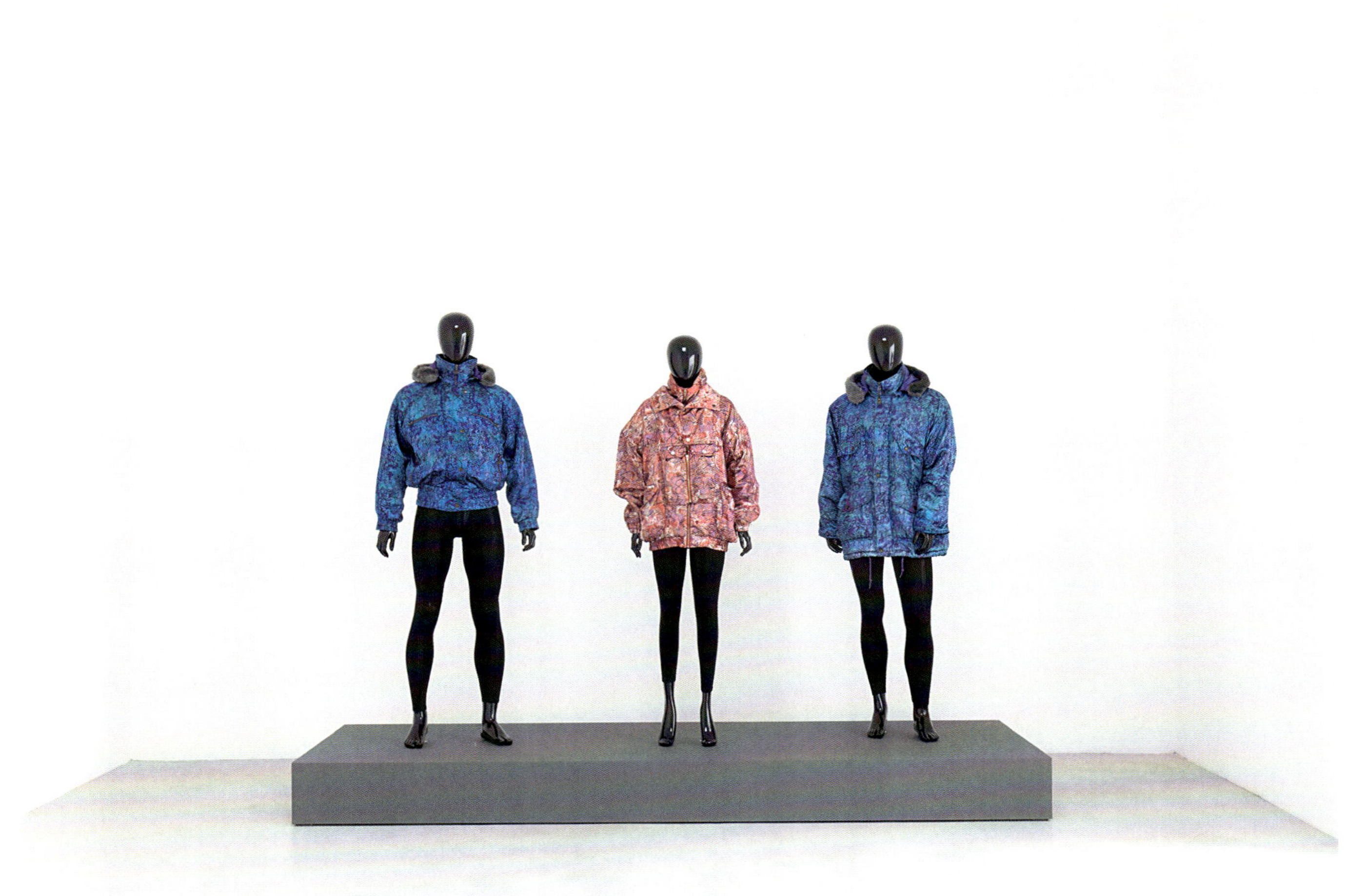

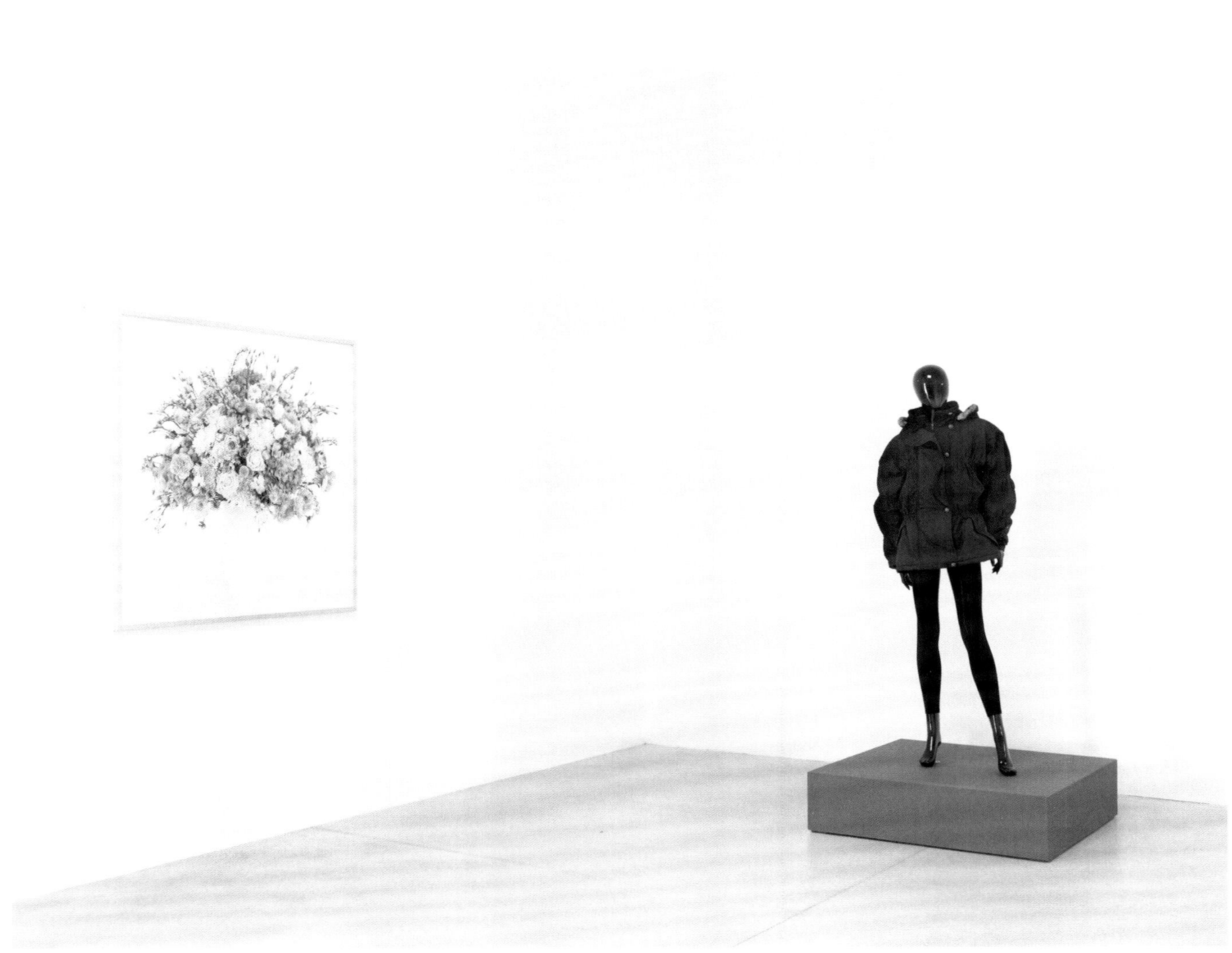

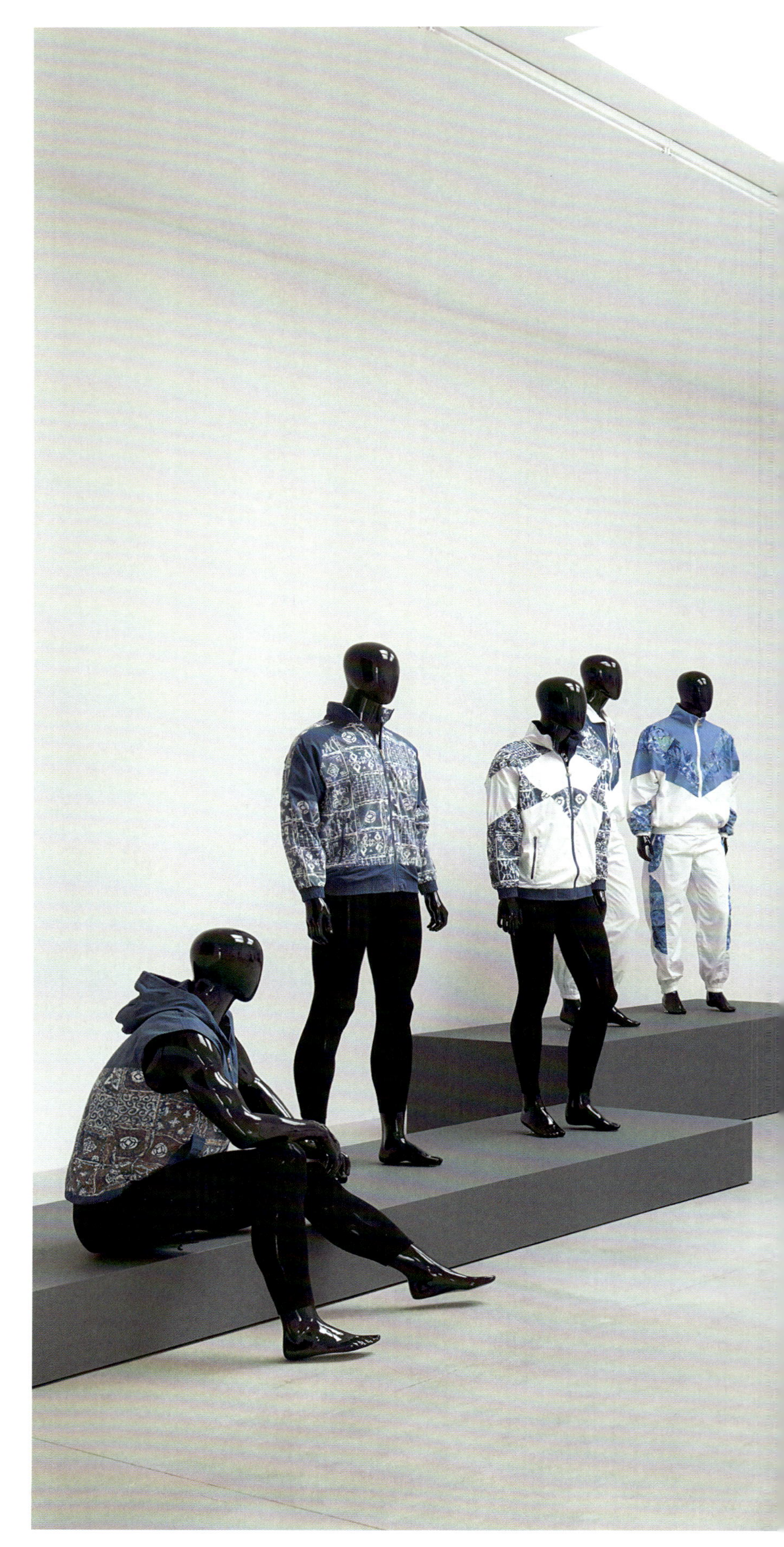

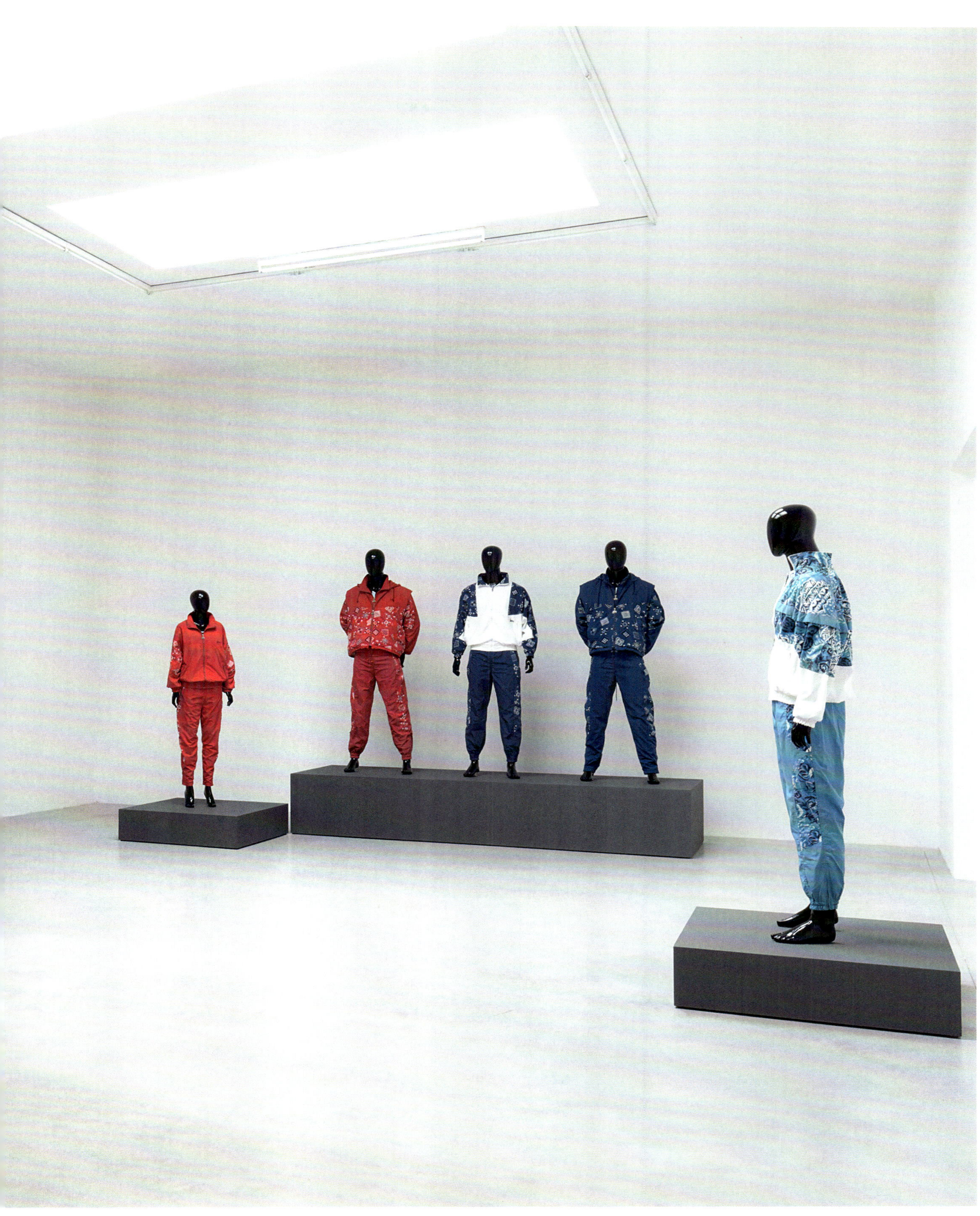

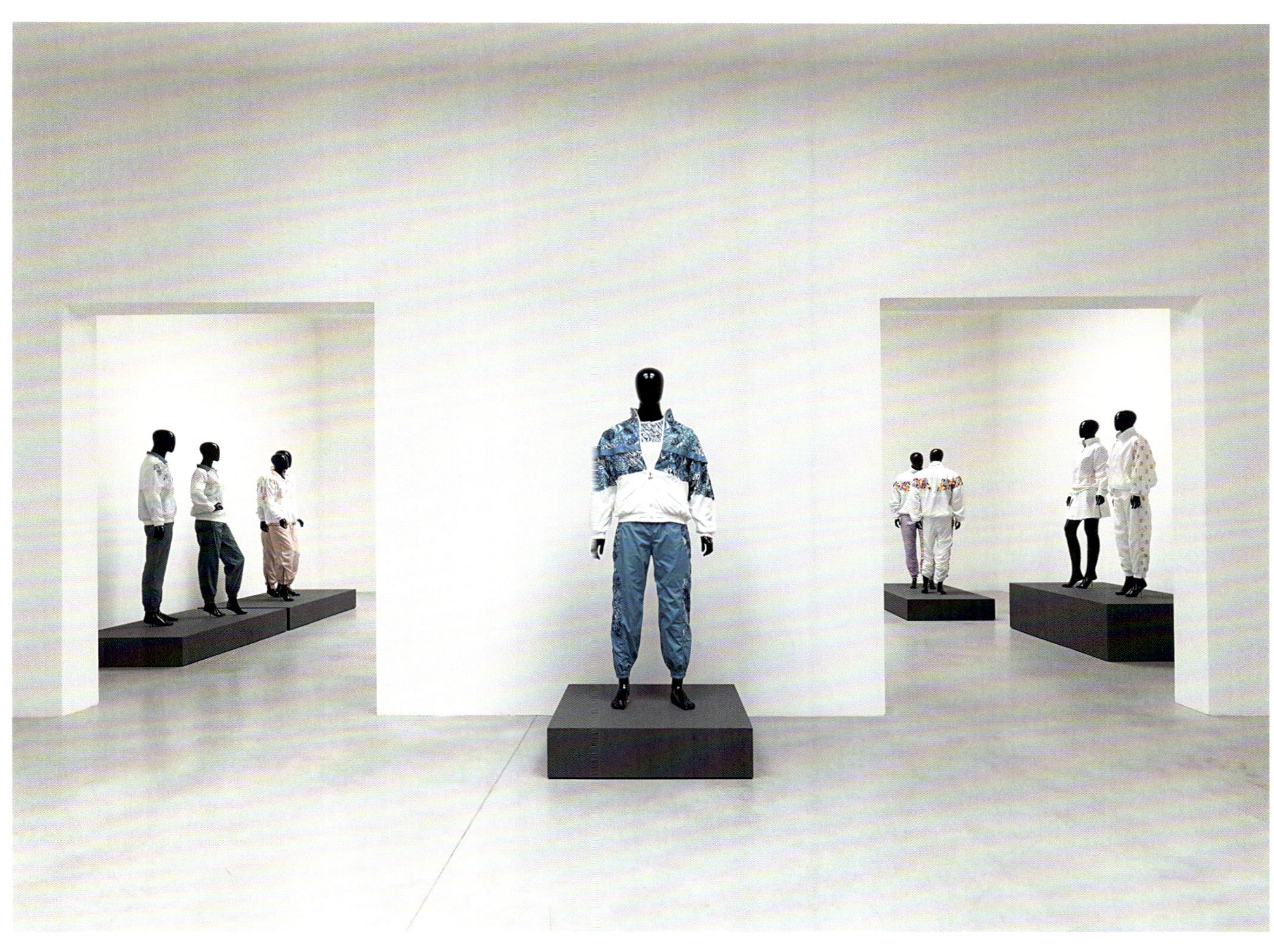

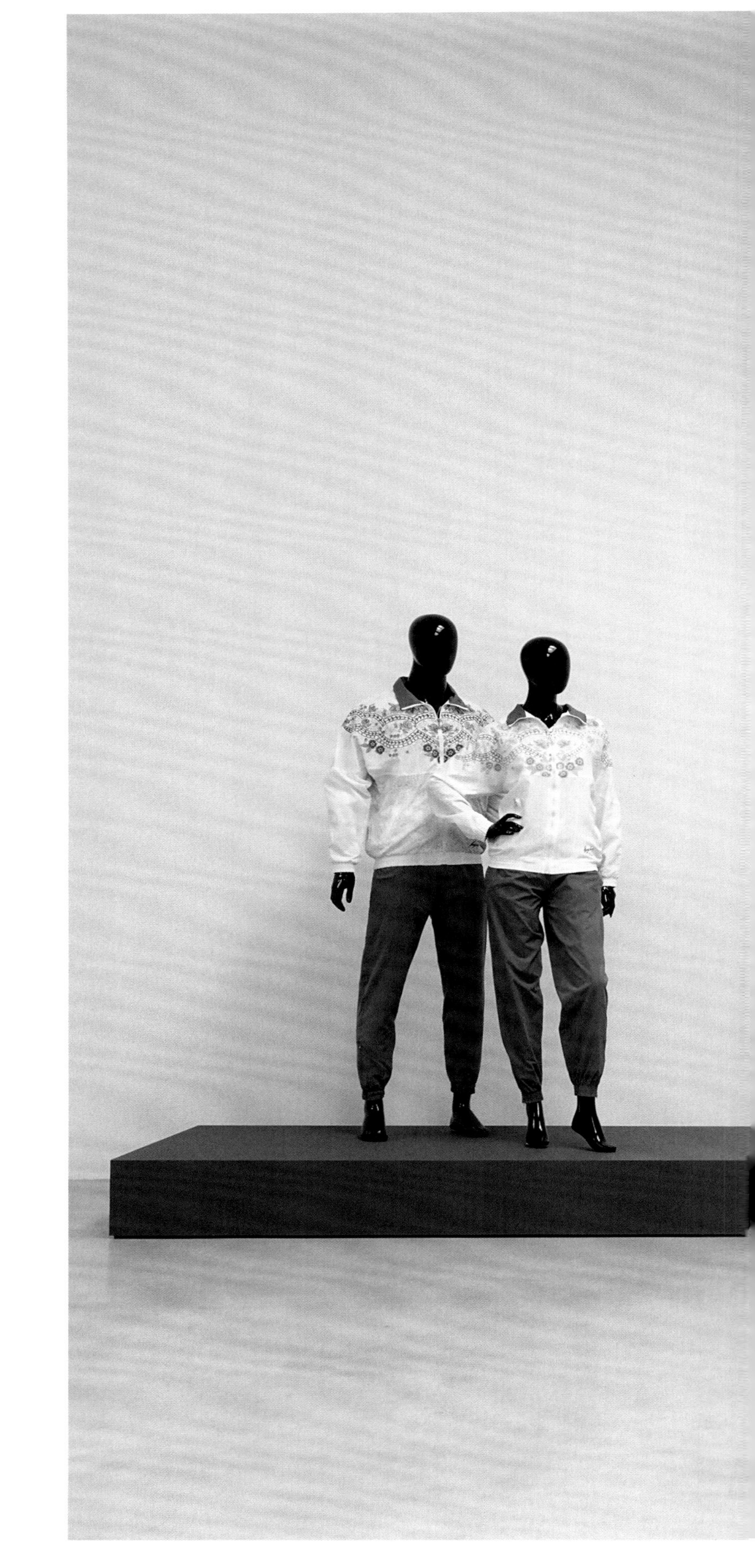

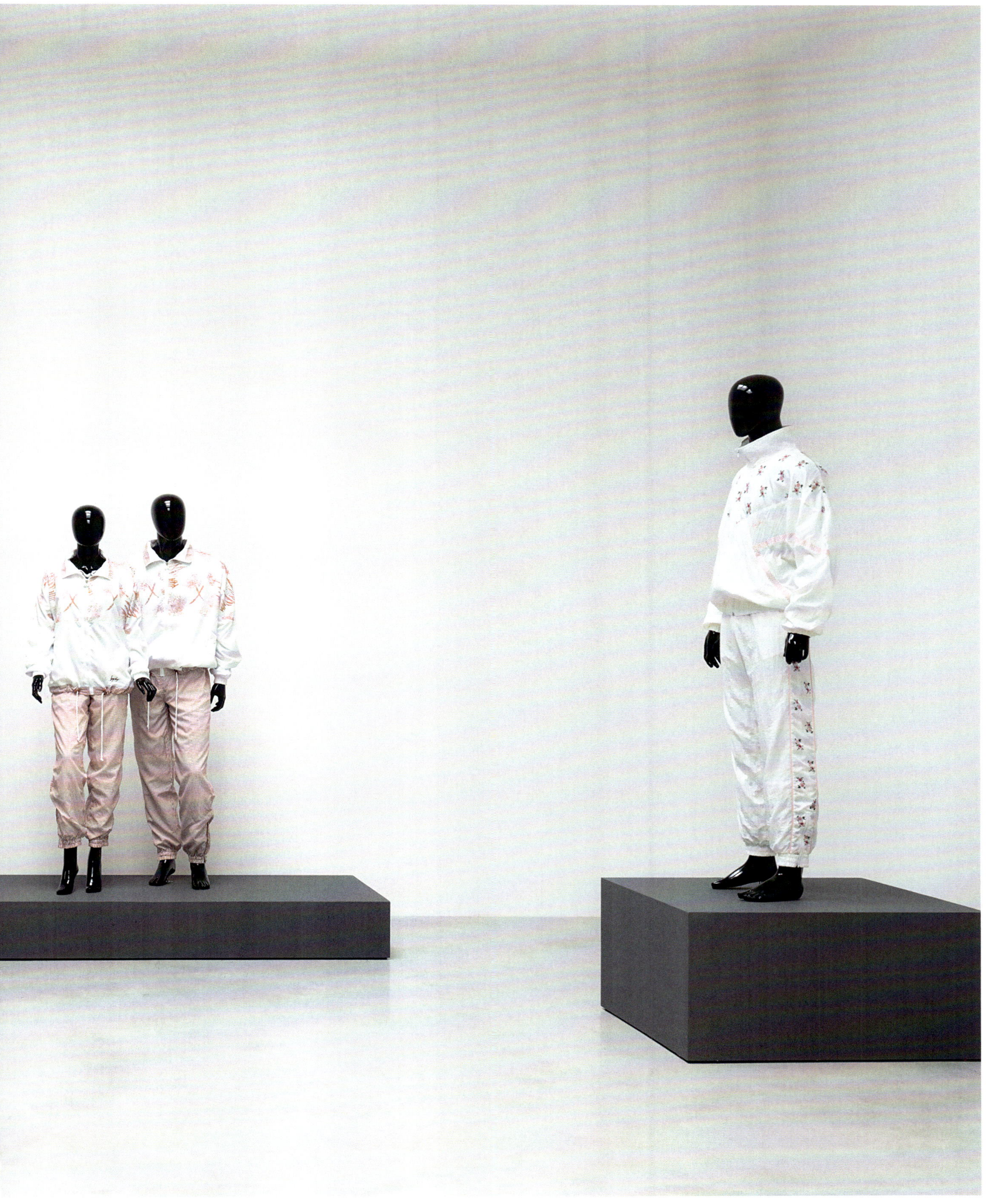

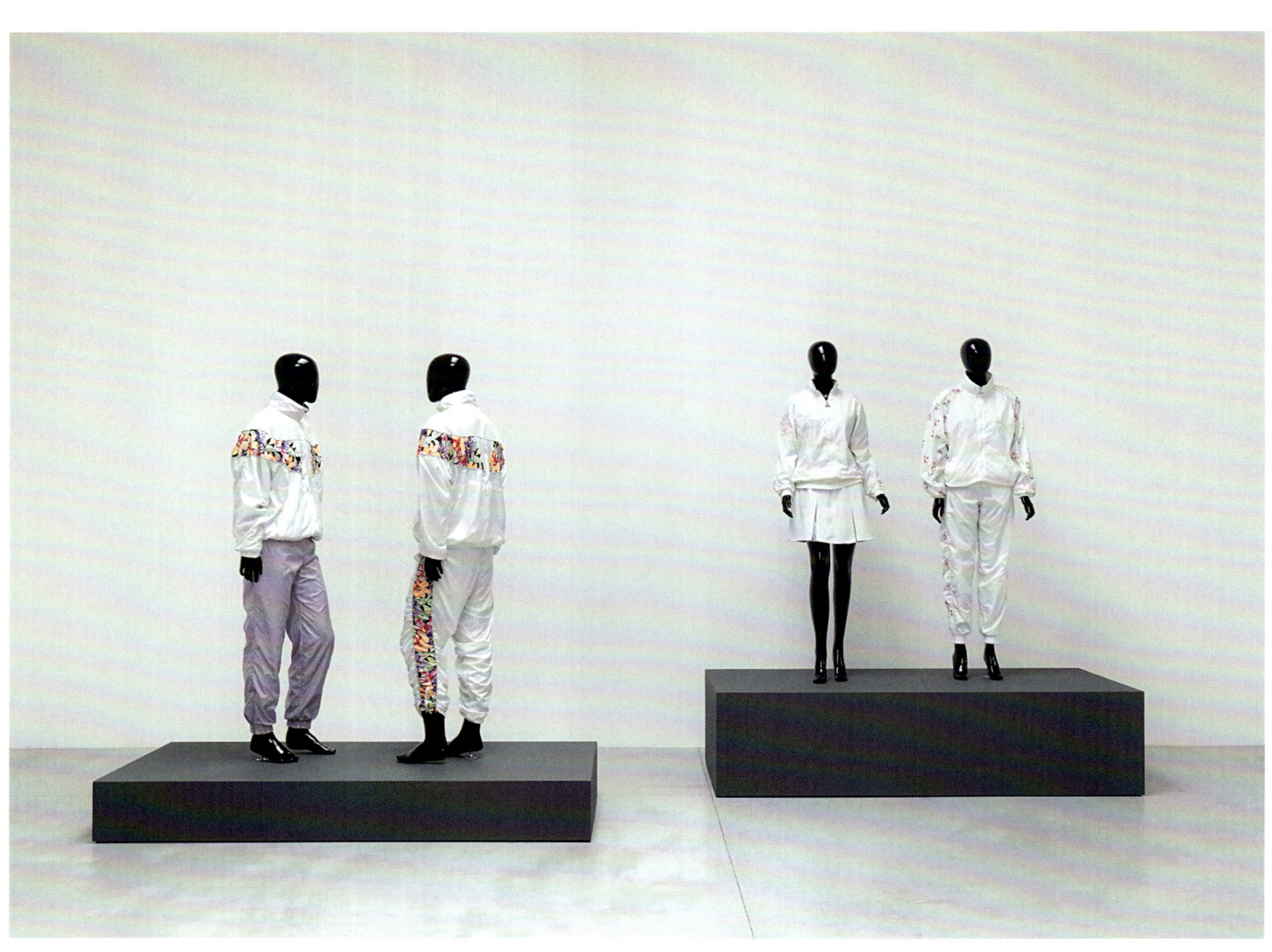

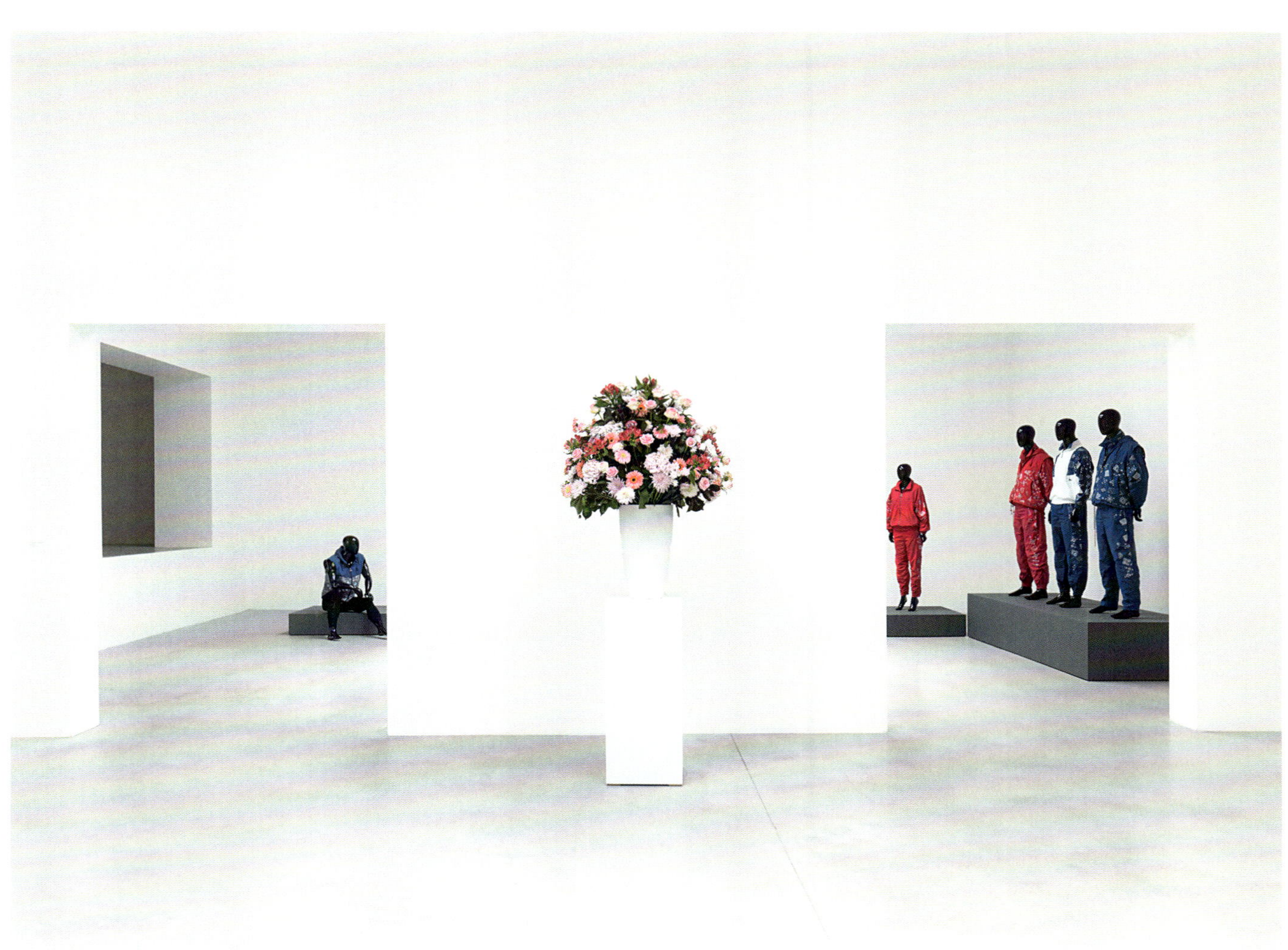

Catalogue

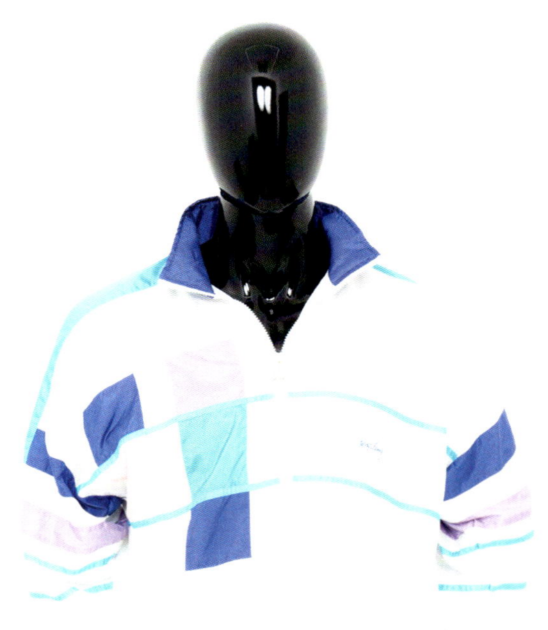

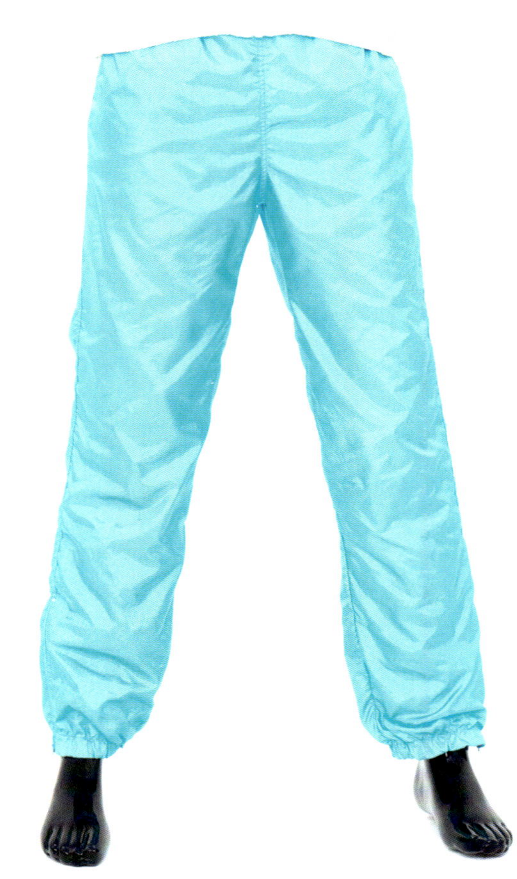

Cat. no. 01

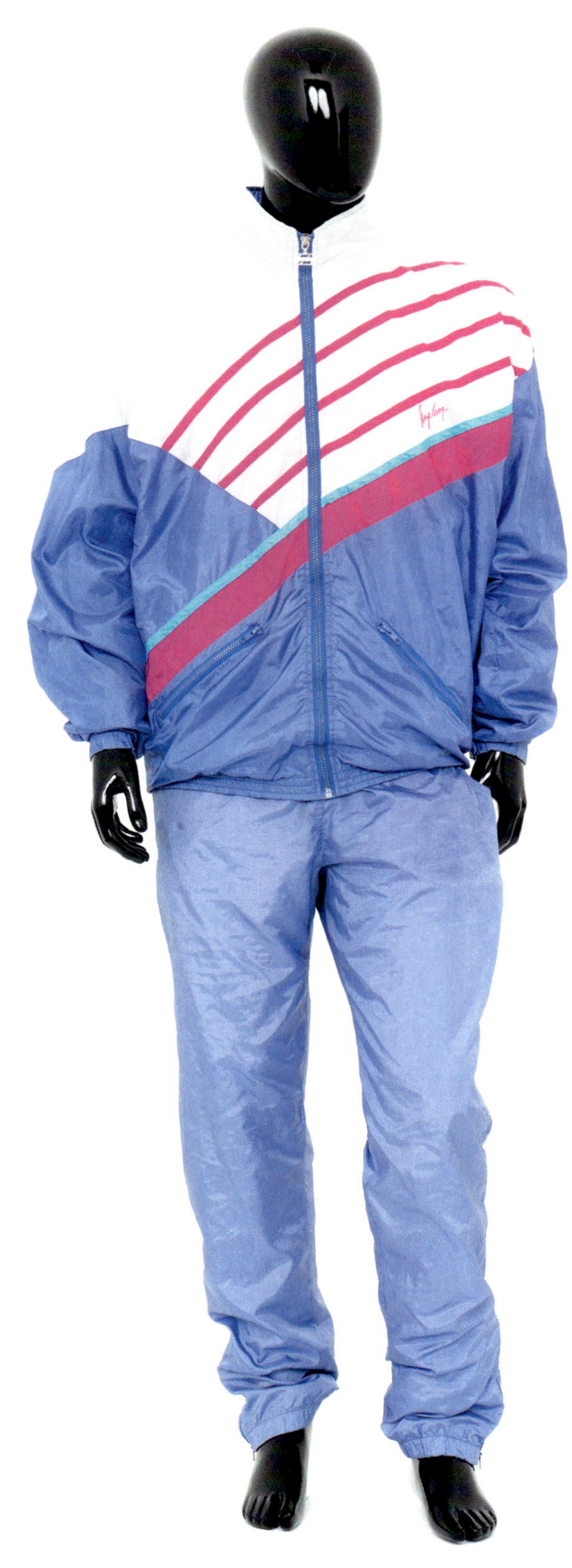

Cat. no. 02

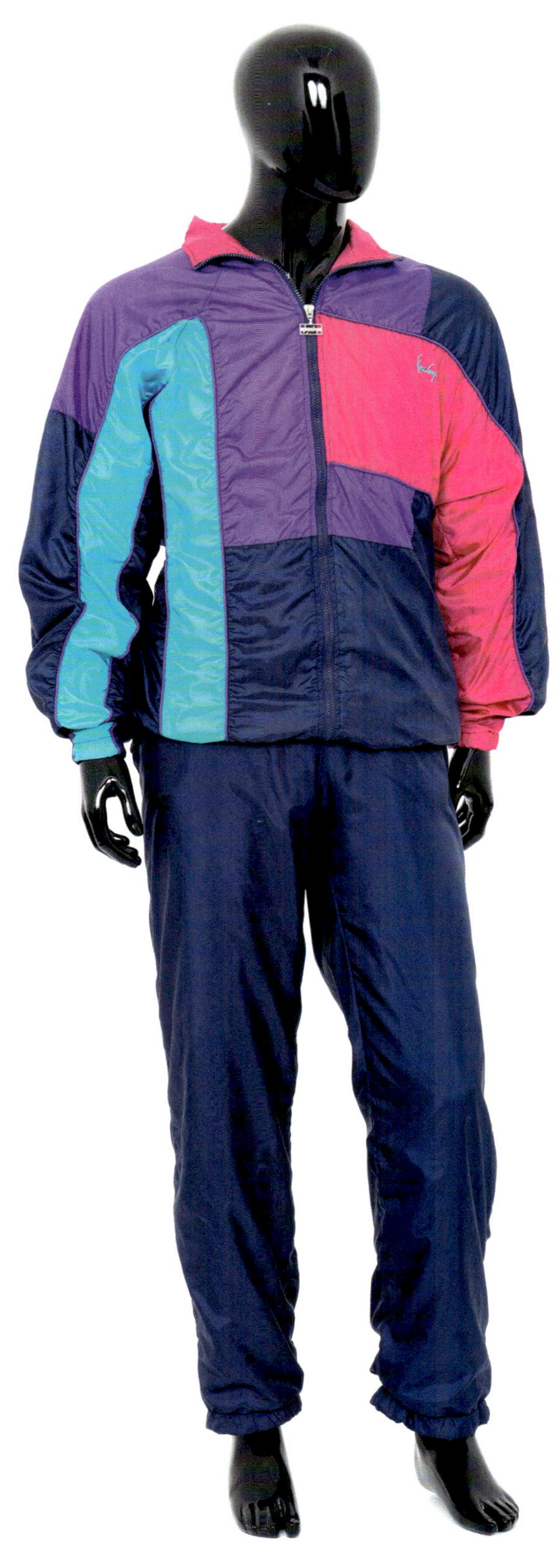

Cat. no. 03

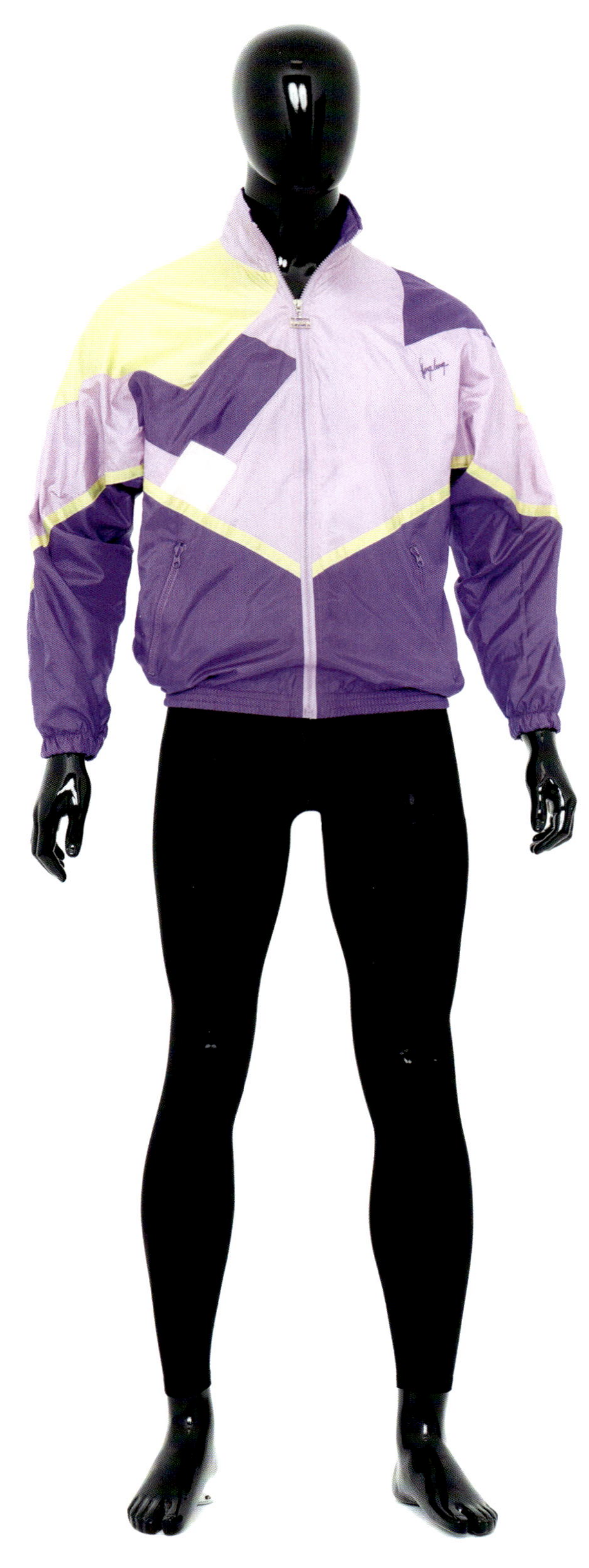

Cat. no. 04

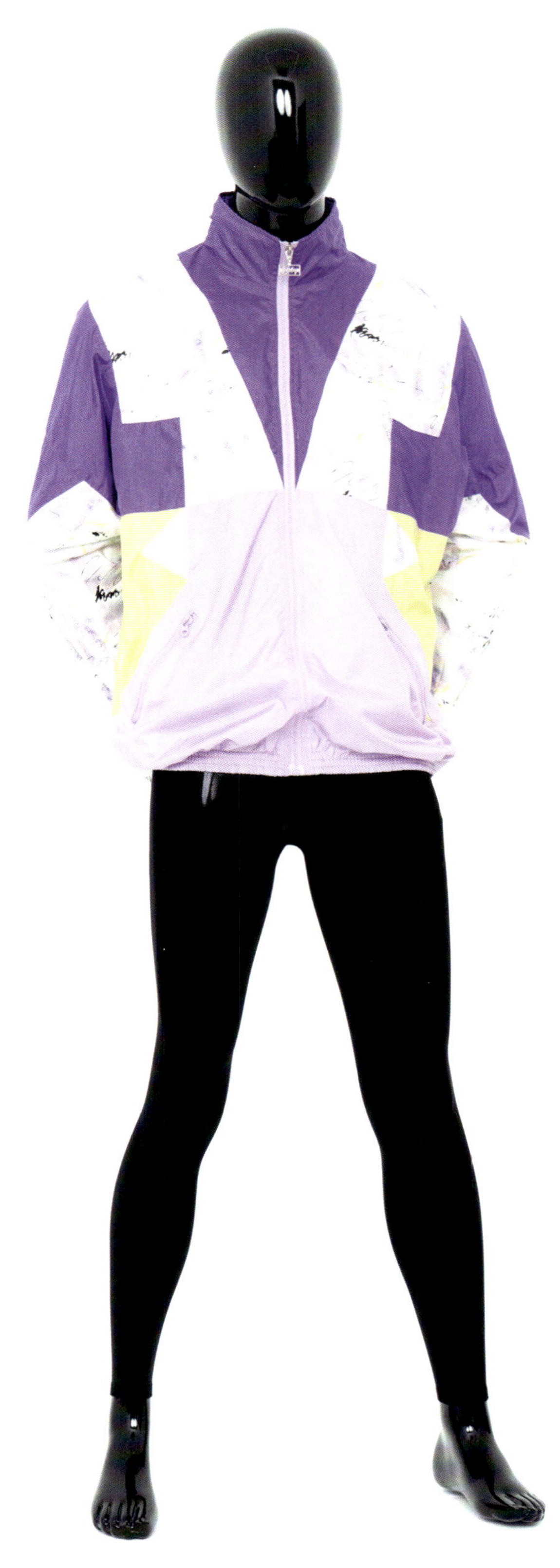

Cat. no. 05

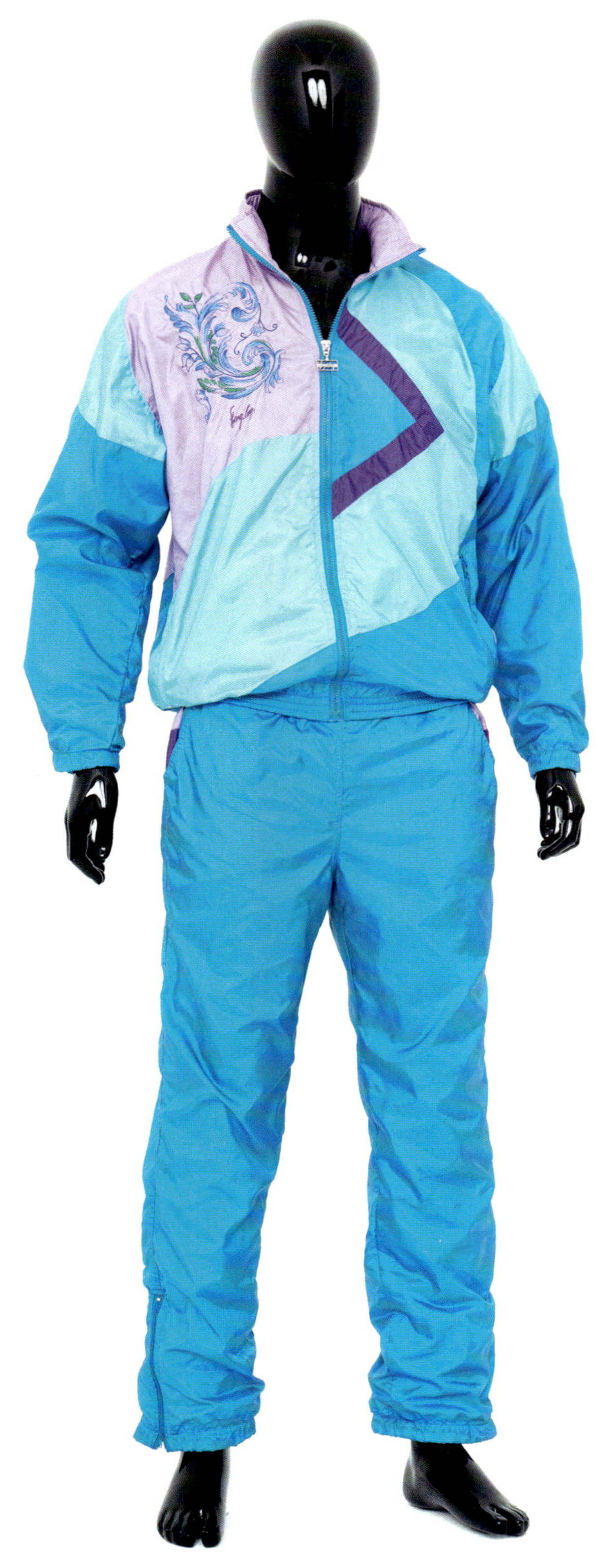

Cat. no. 06

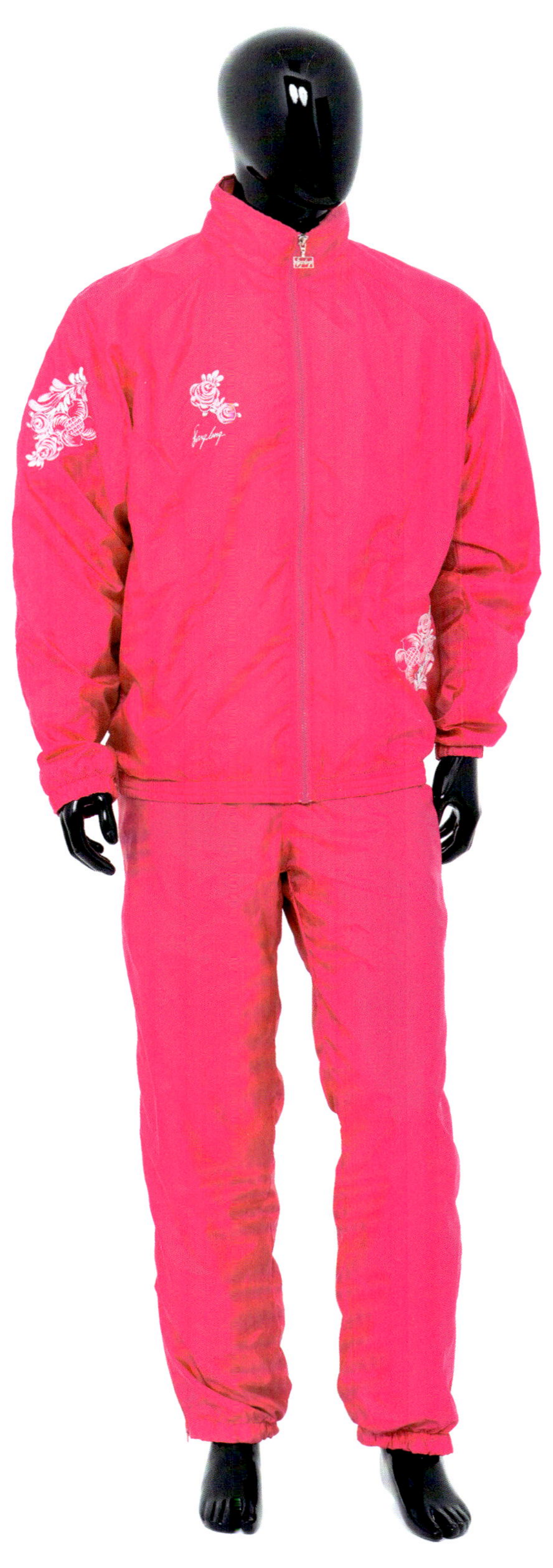

Cat. no. 07

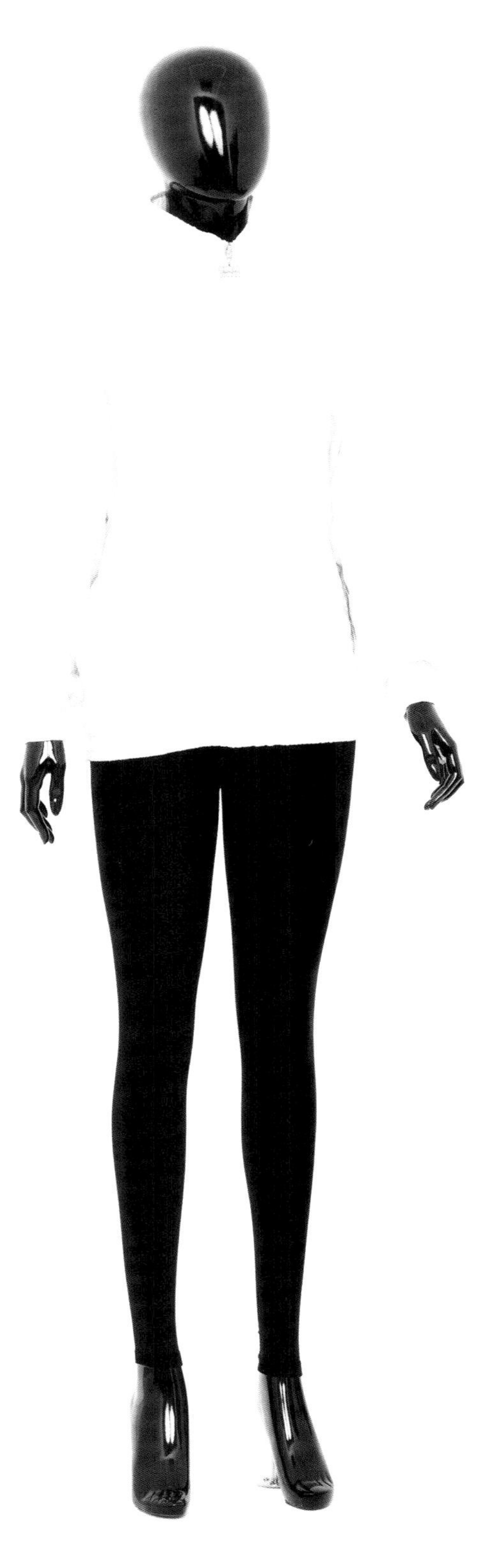

Cat. no. 08

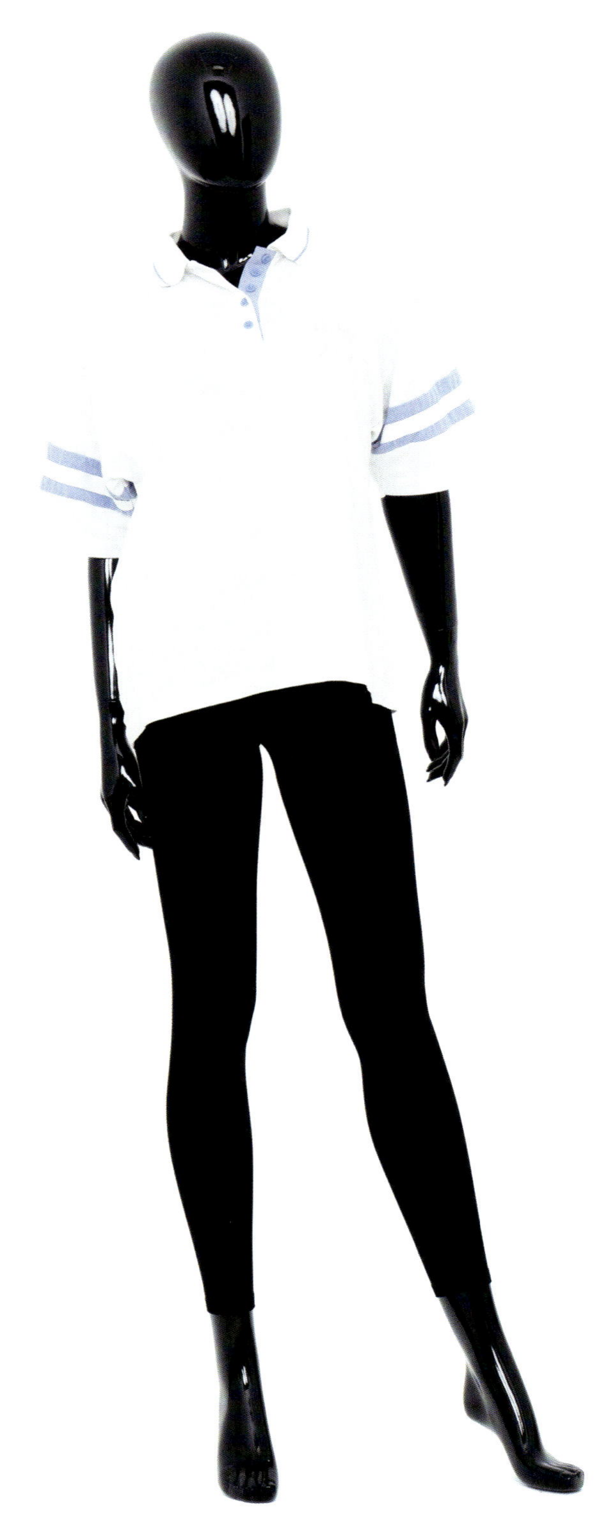

Cat. no. 09

Cat. no. 10

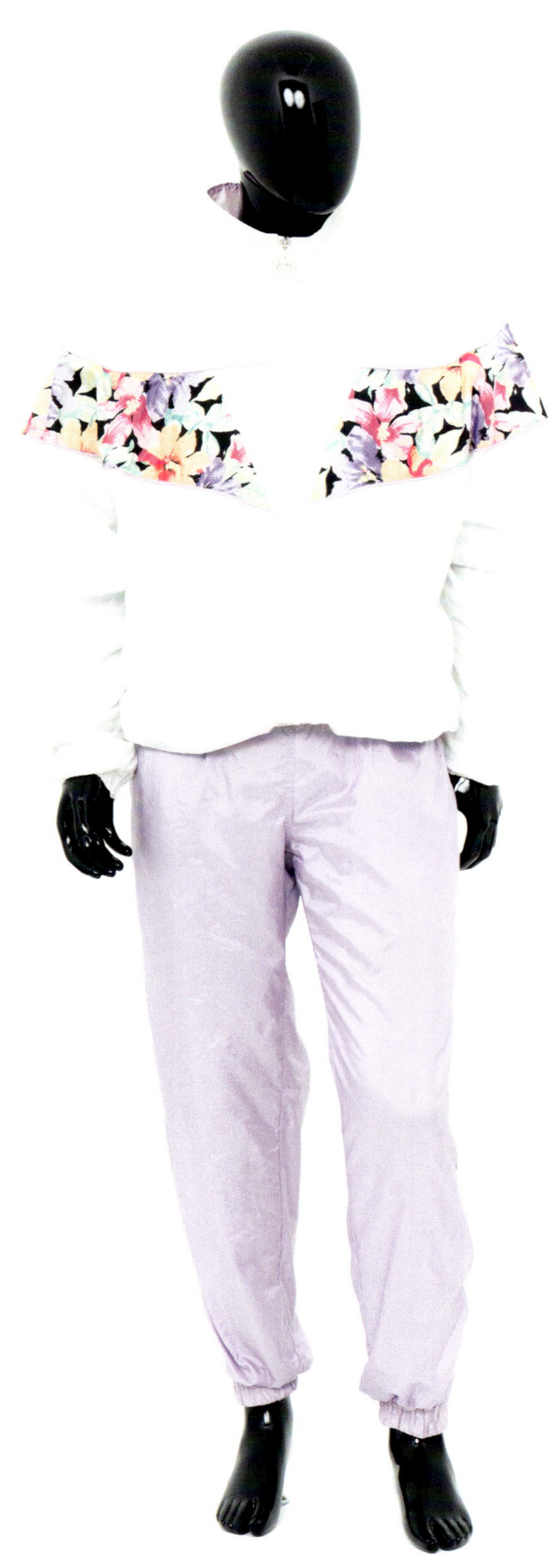

Cat. no. 11

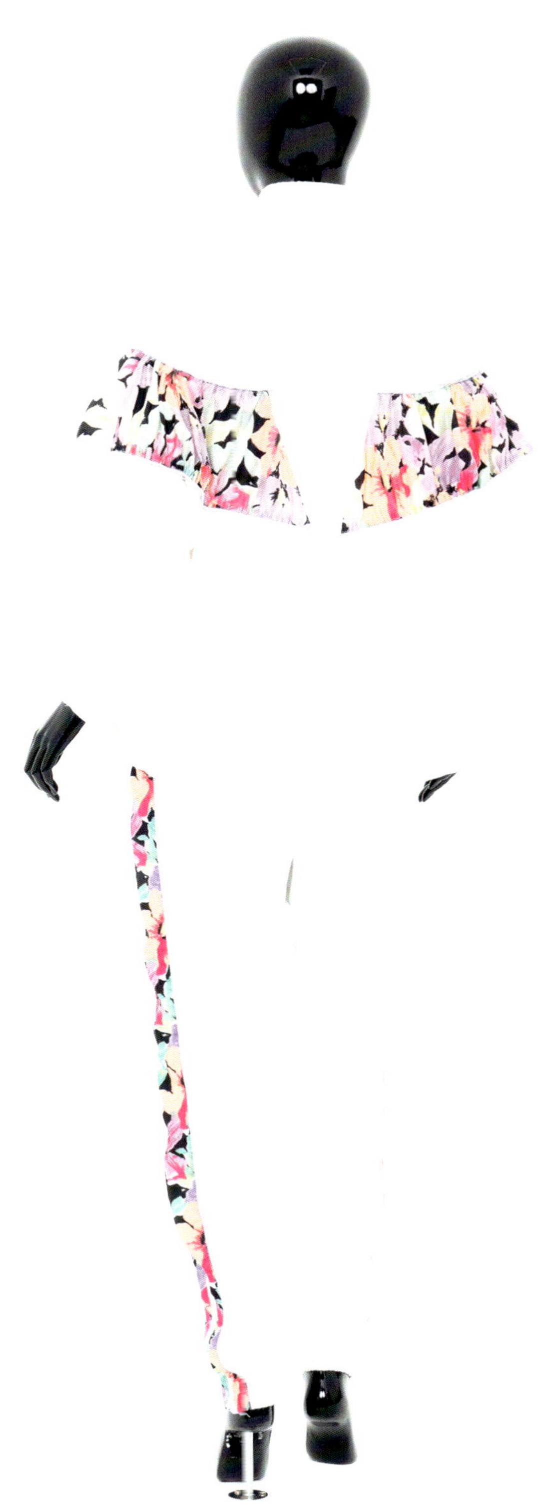

Cat. no. 12

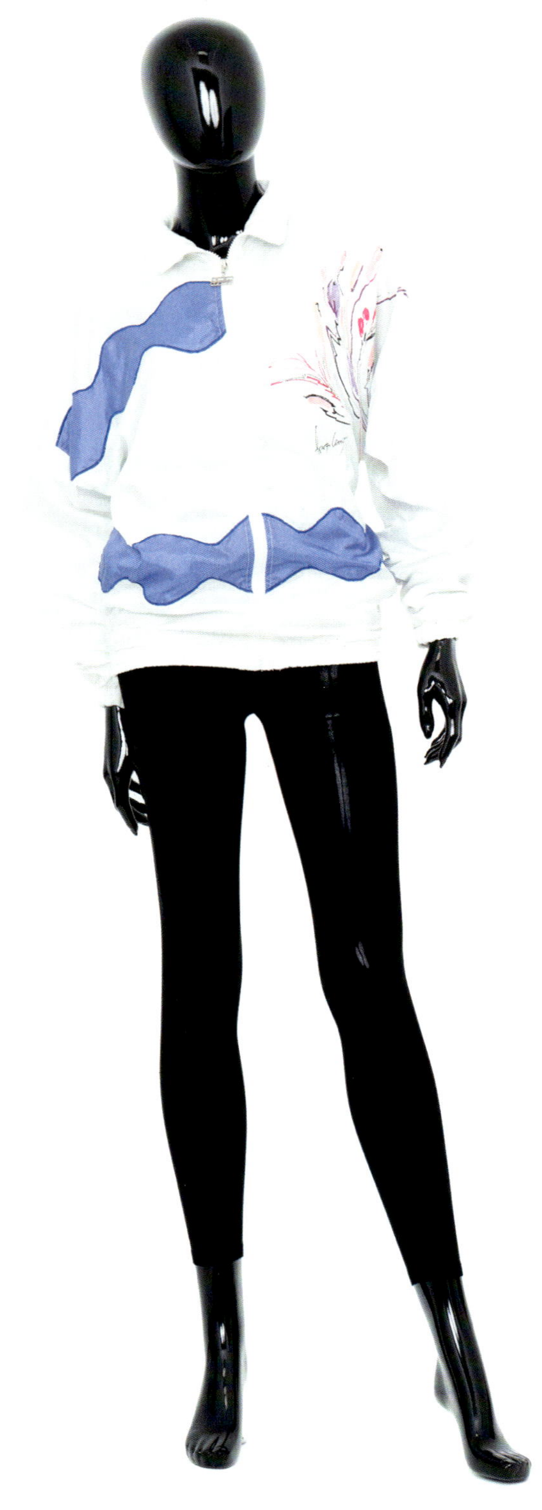

Cat. no. 13

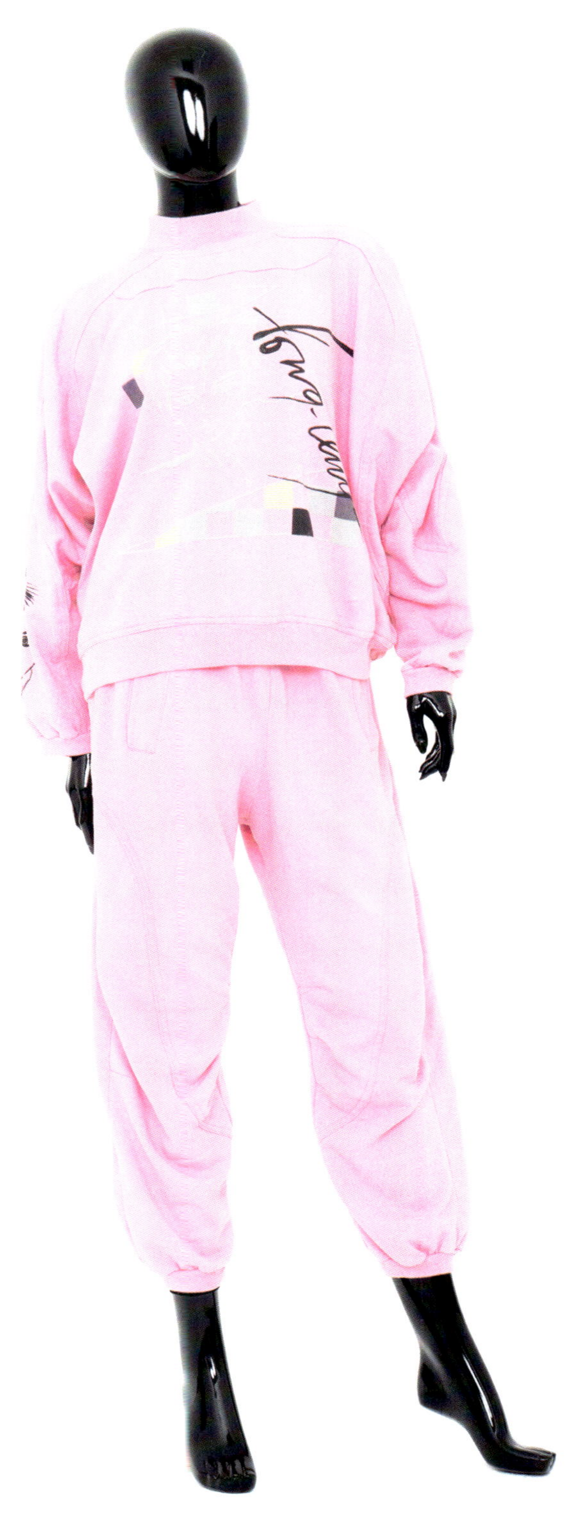

Cat. no. 14

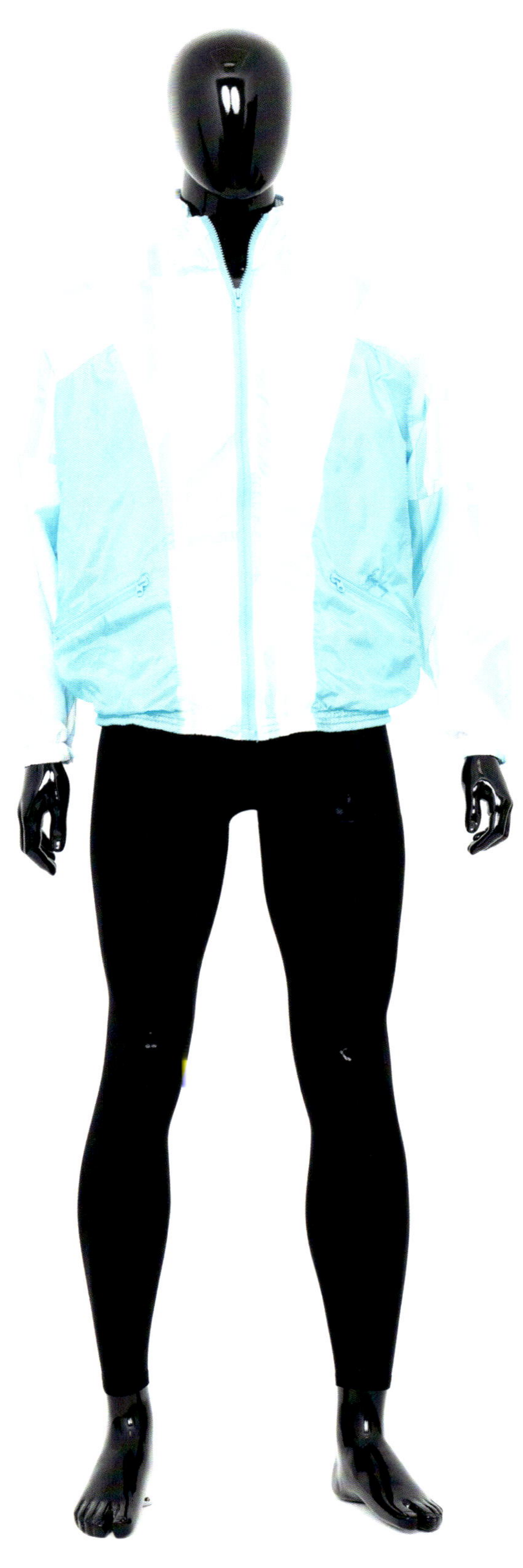

Cat. no. 15

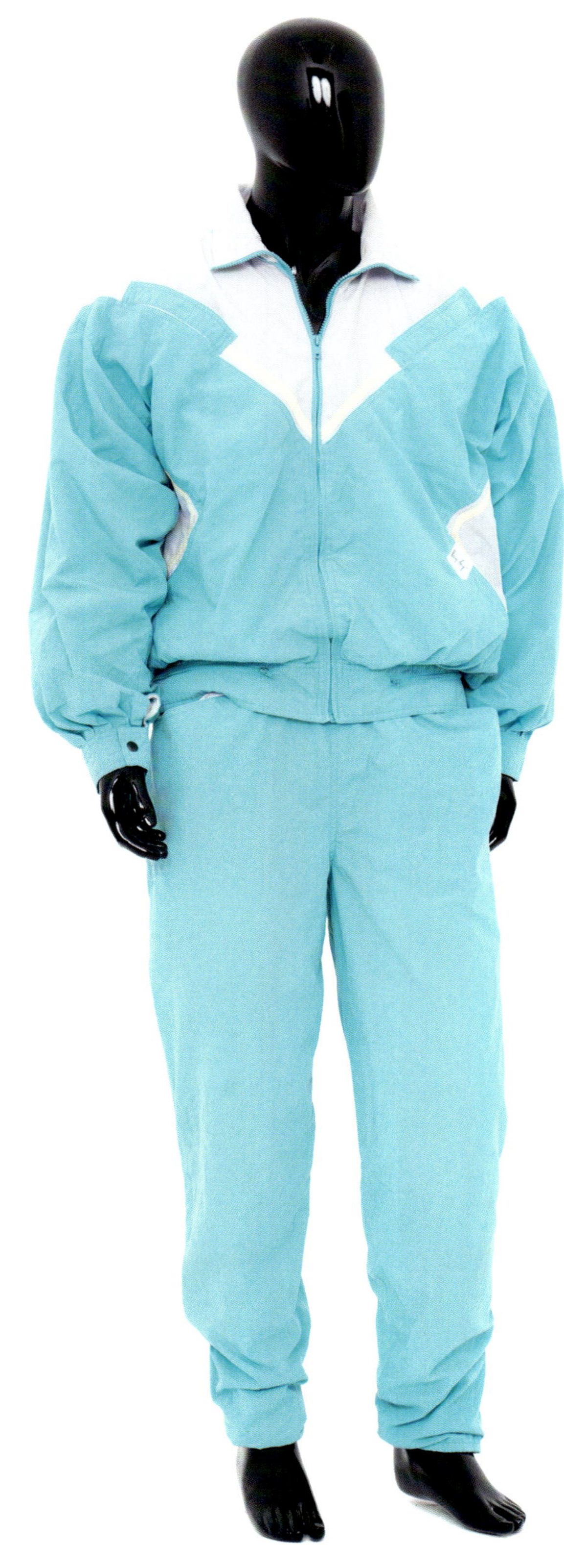

Cat. no. 16

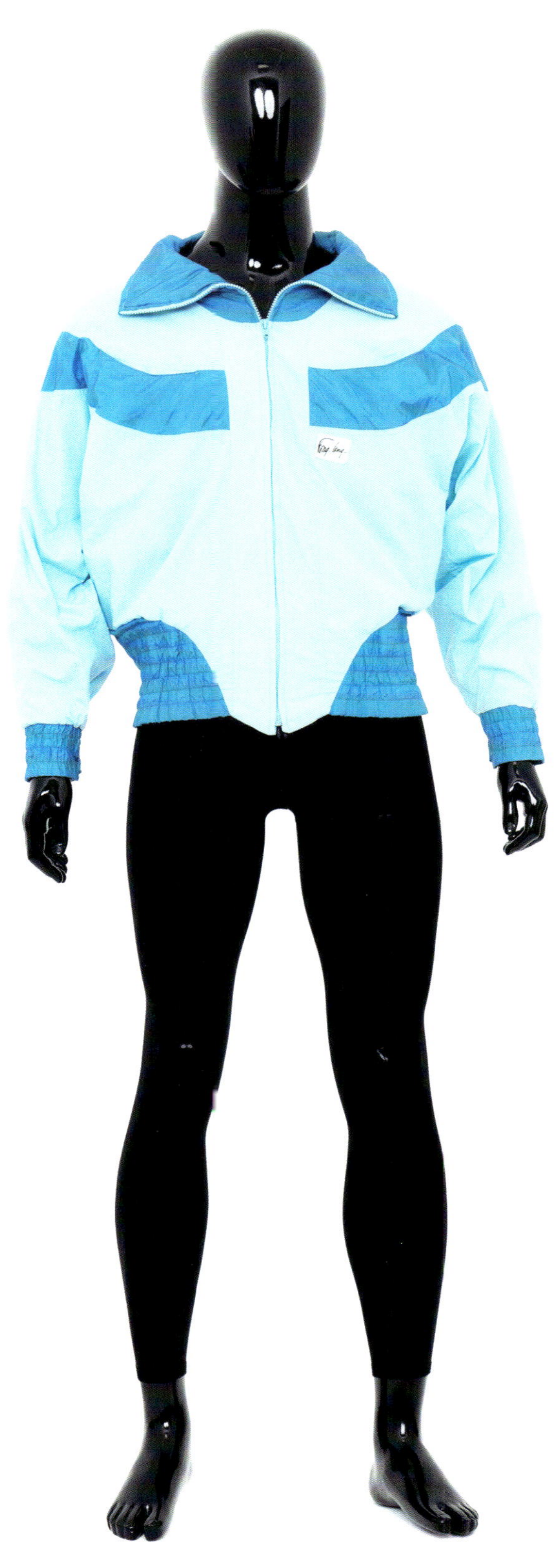

Cat. no. 17

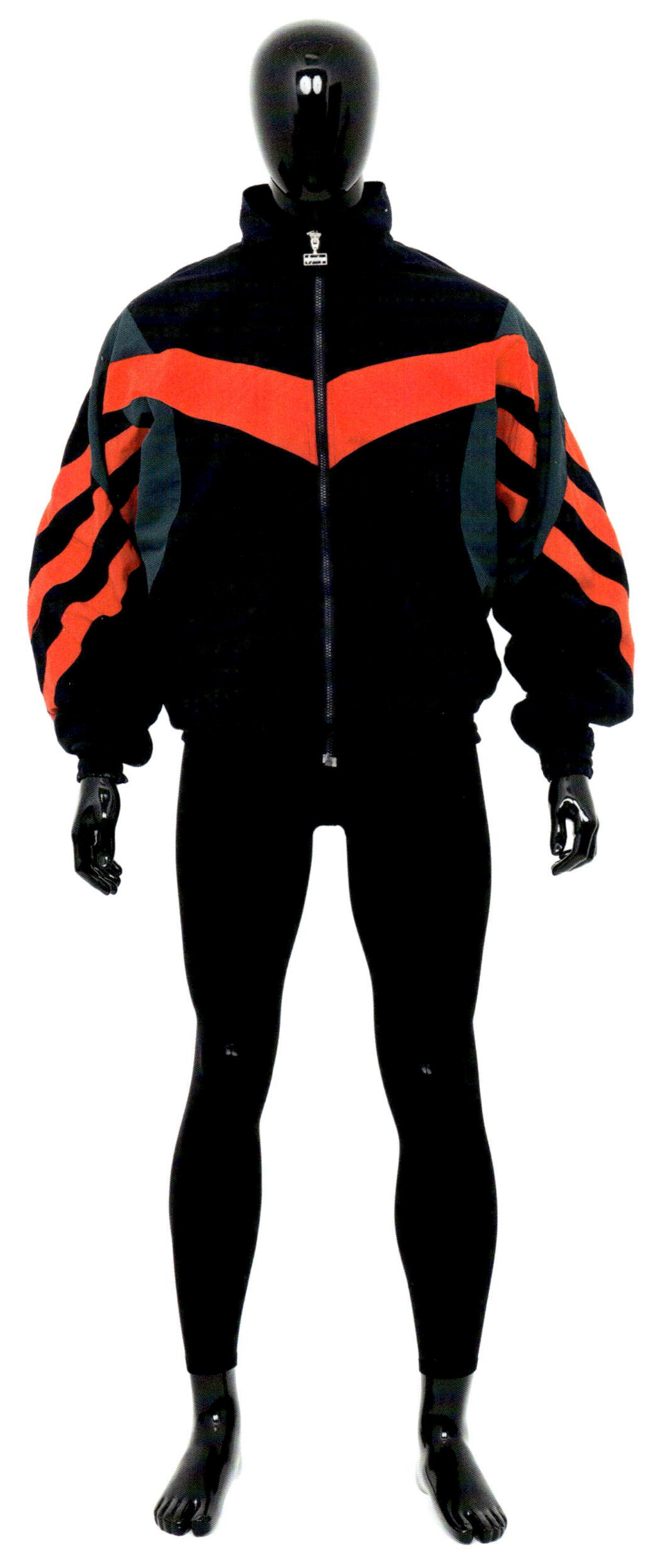

Cat. no. 18

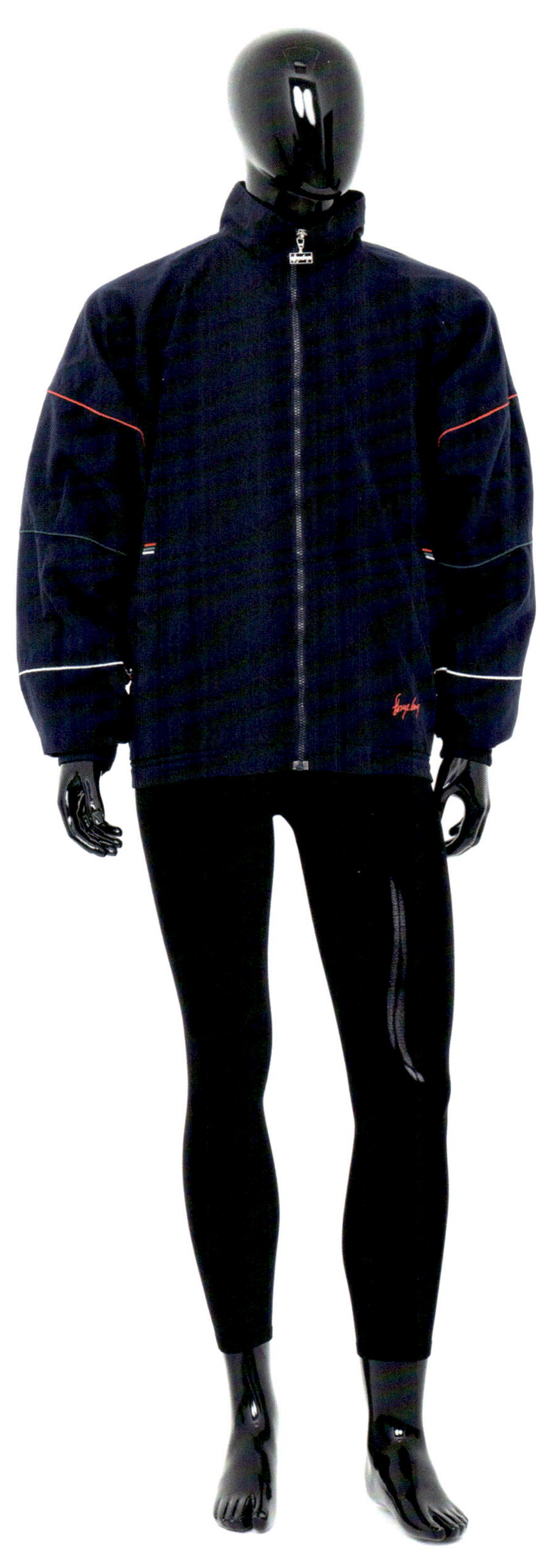

Cat. no. 19

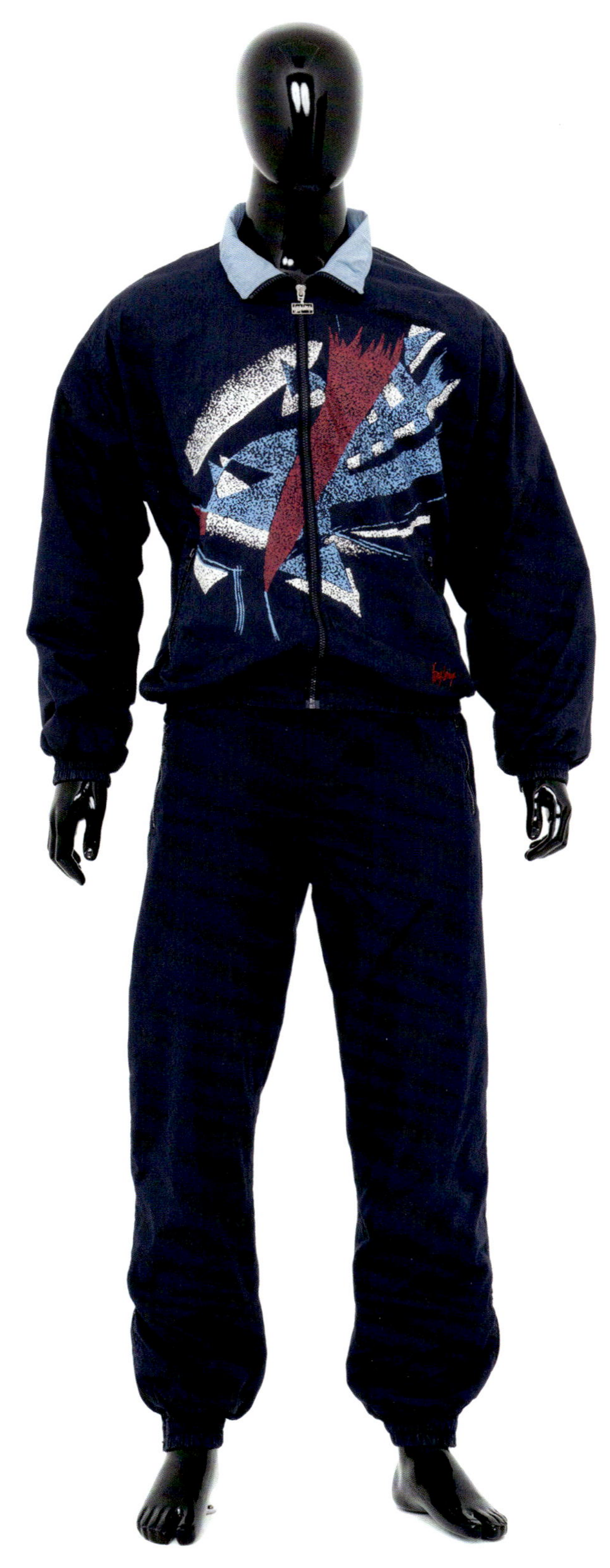

Cat. no. 20

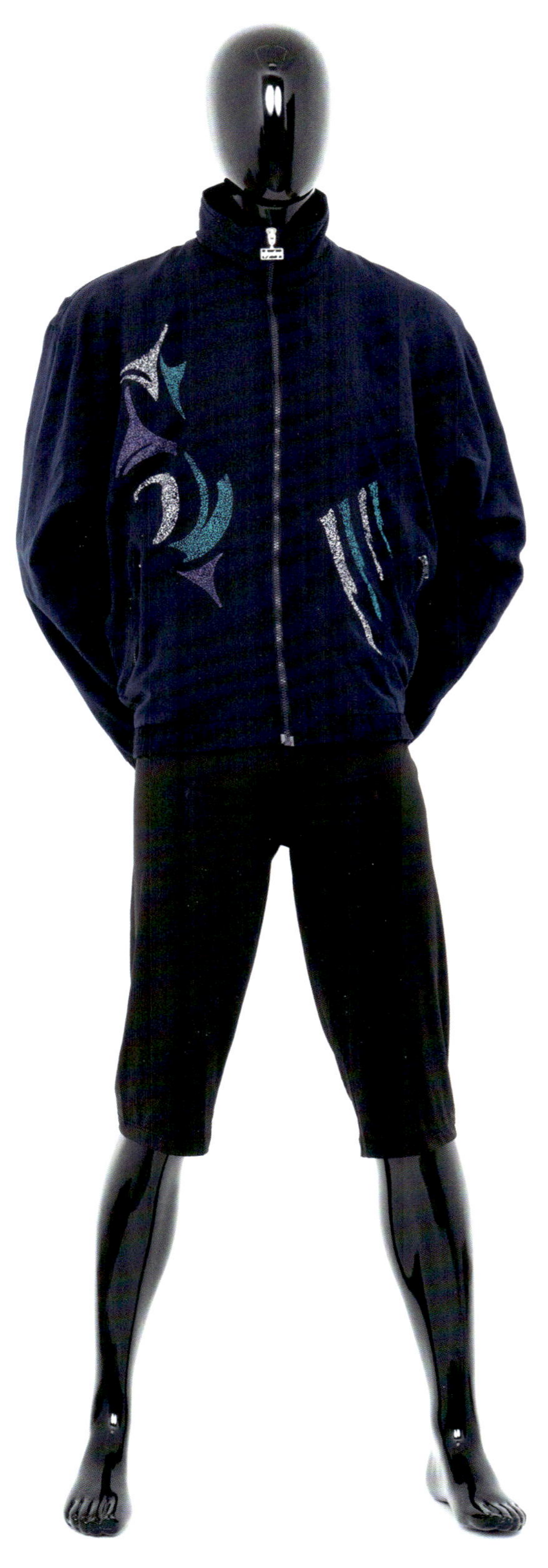

Cat. no. 21

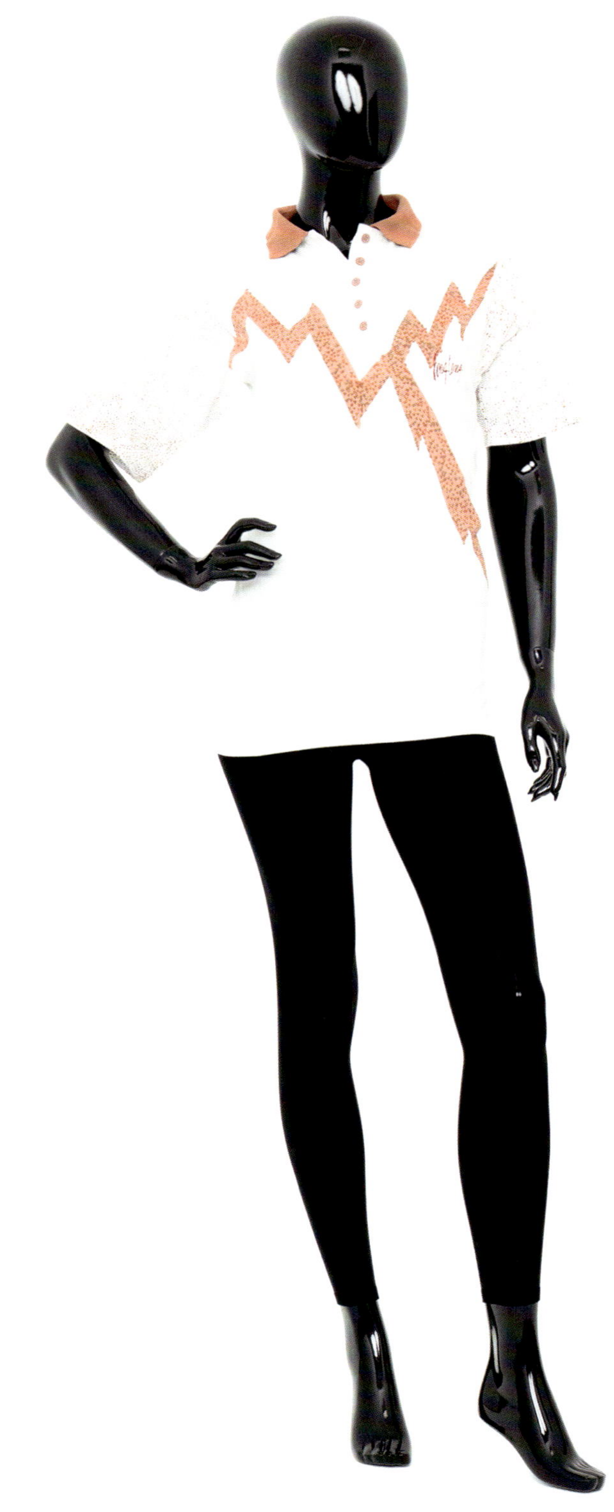

Cat. no. 22

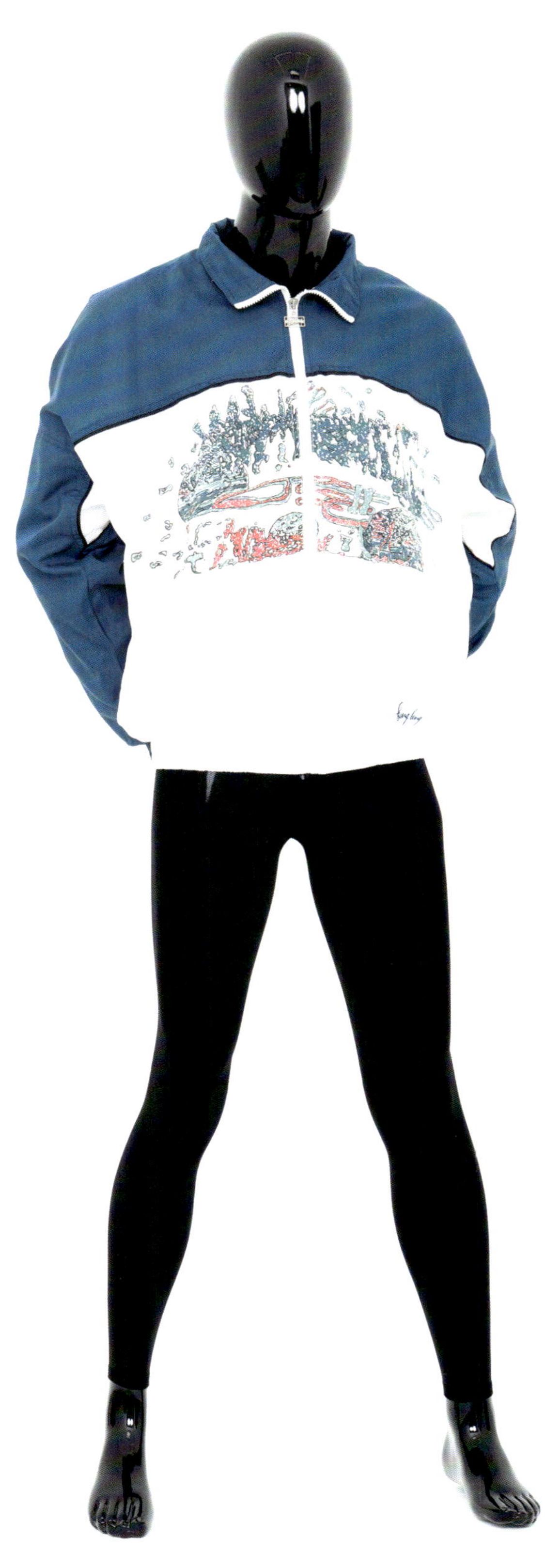

Cat. no. 23

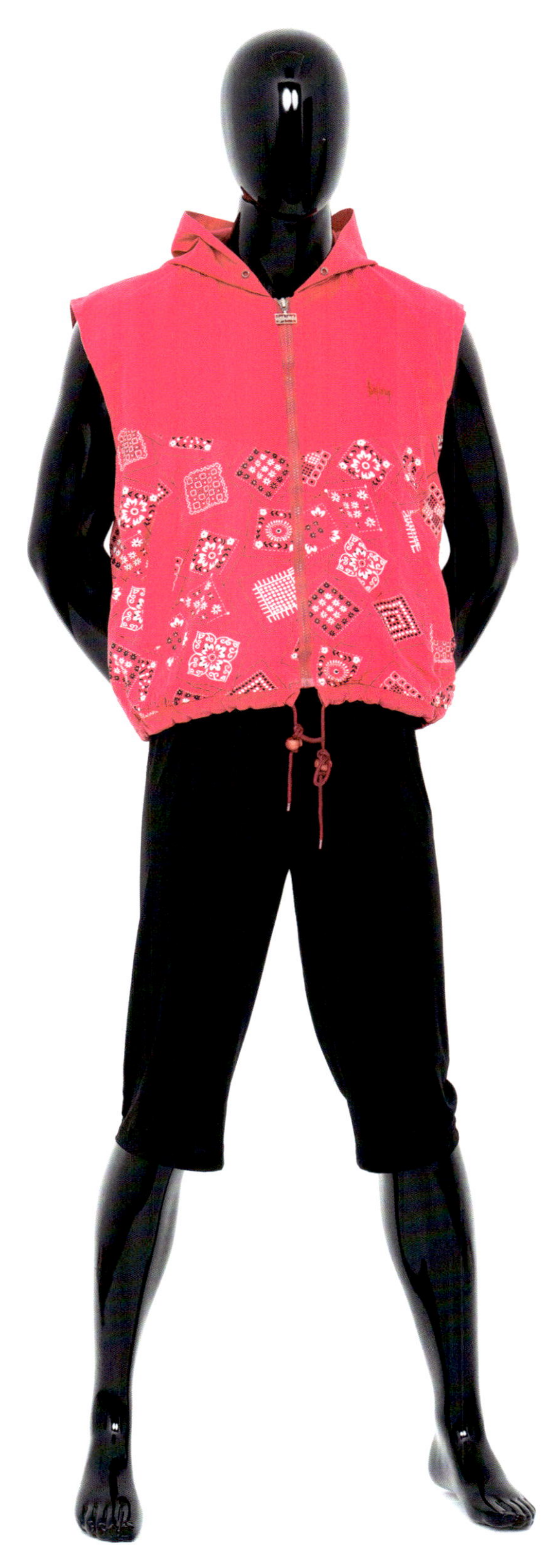

Cat. no. 24

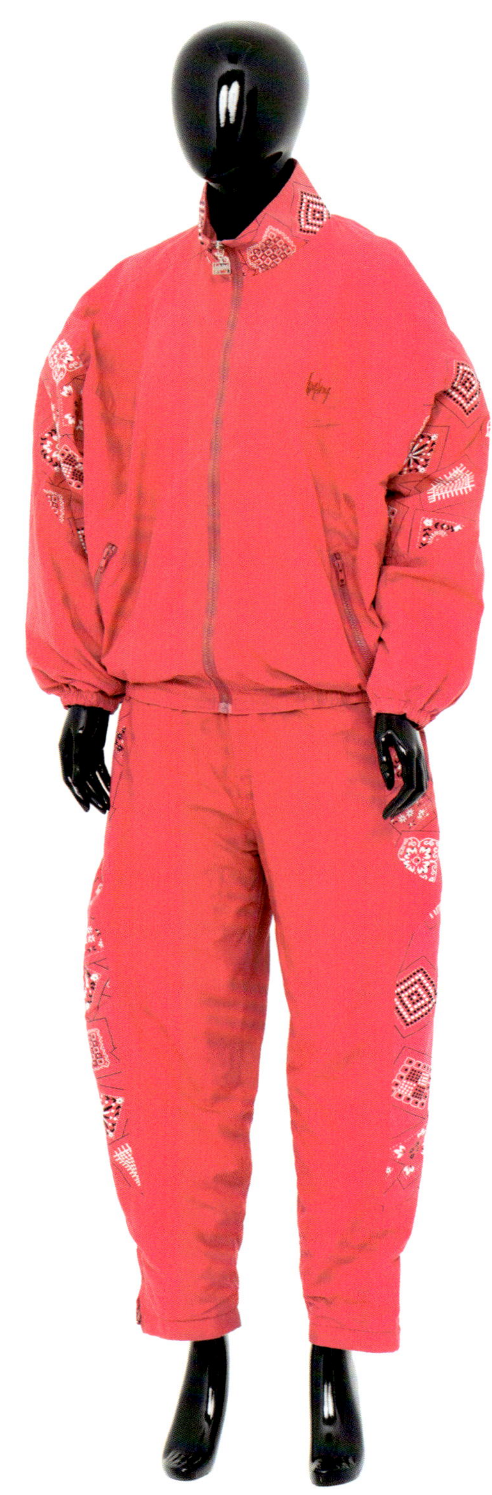

Cat. no. 25

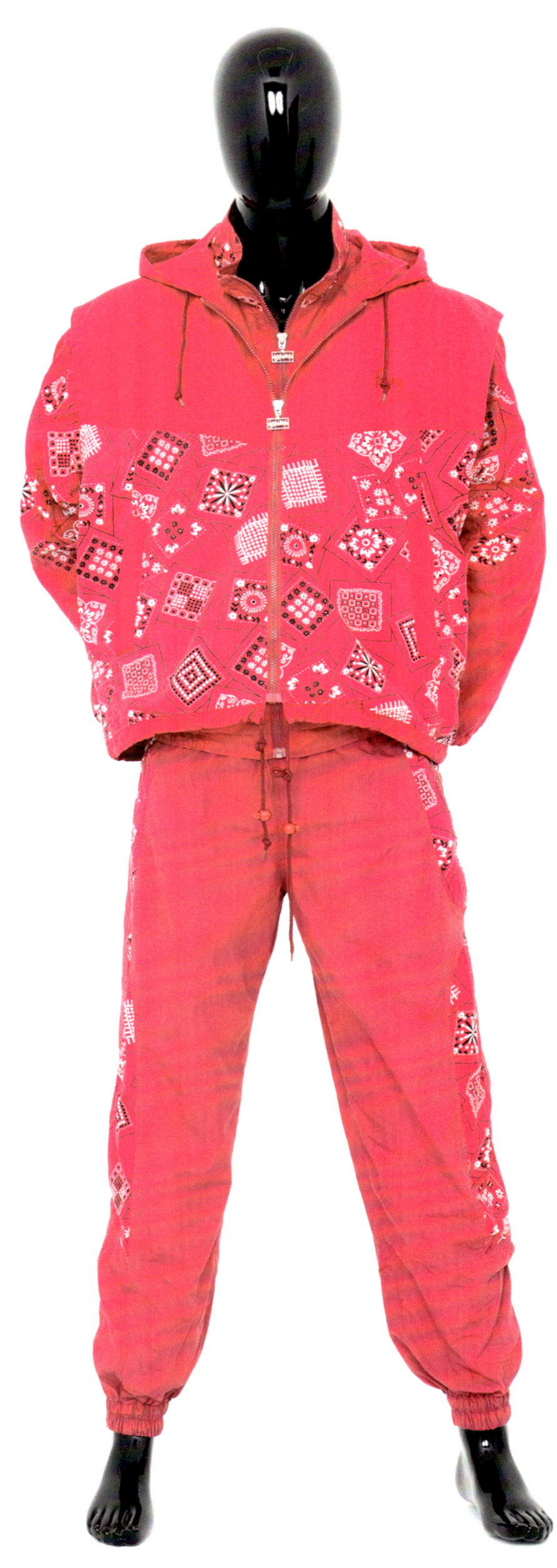

Cat. no. 26

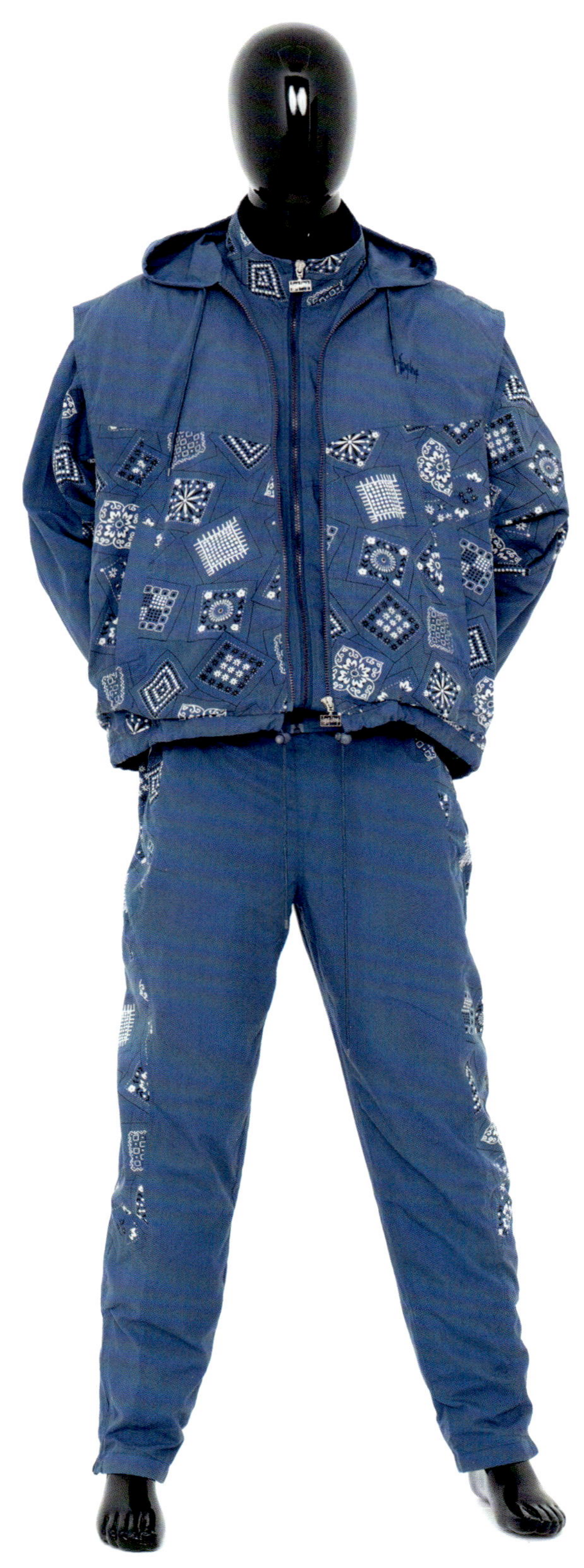

Cat. no. 27

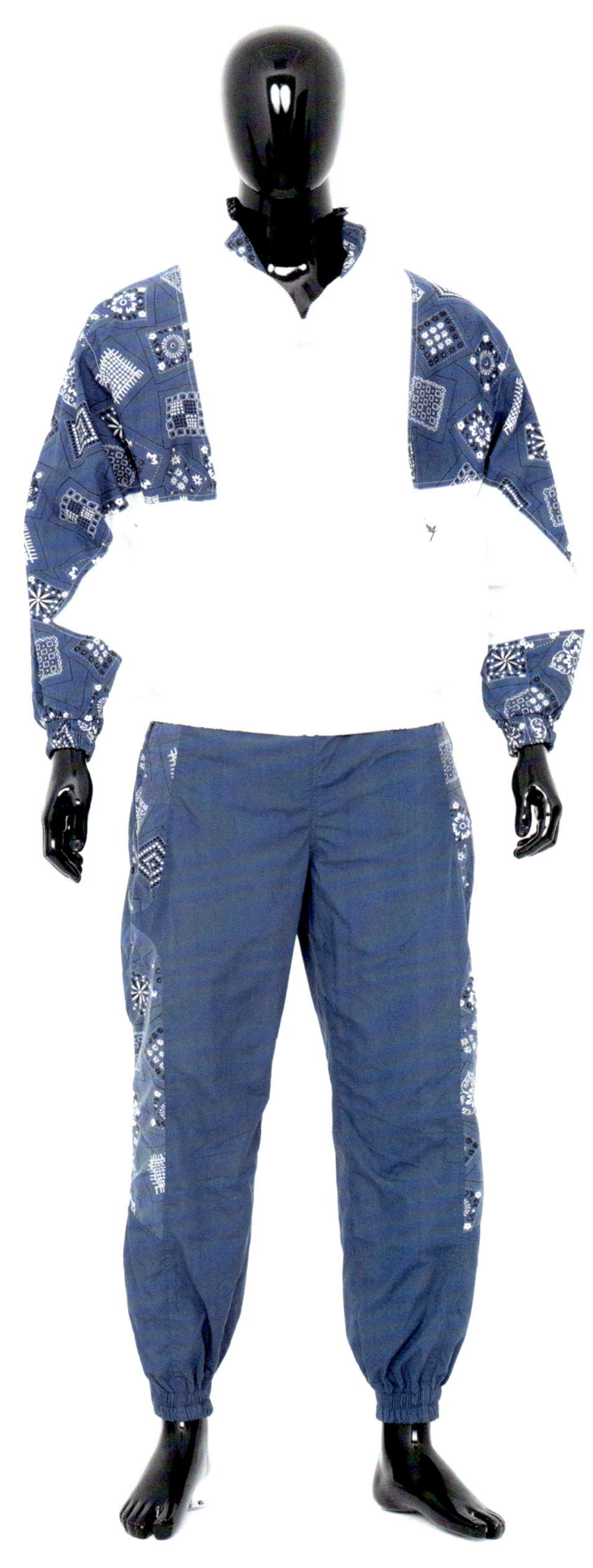

Cat. no. 28

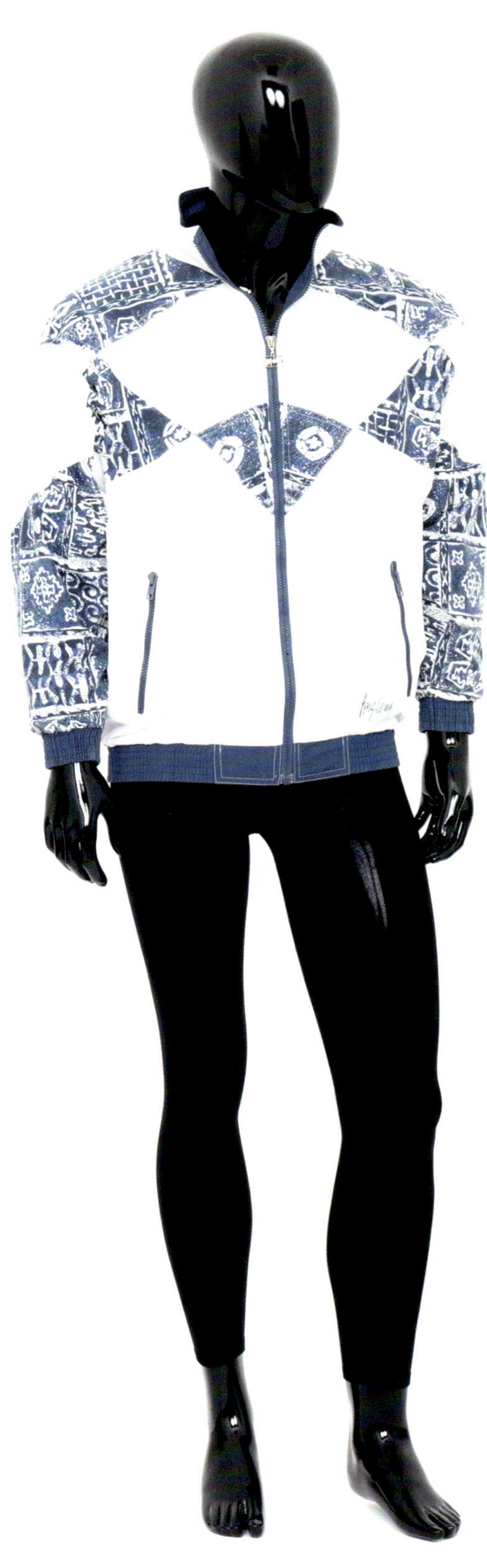

Cat. no. 29

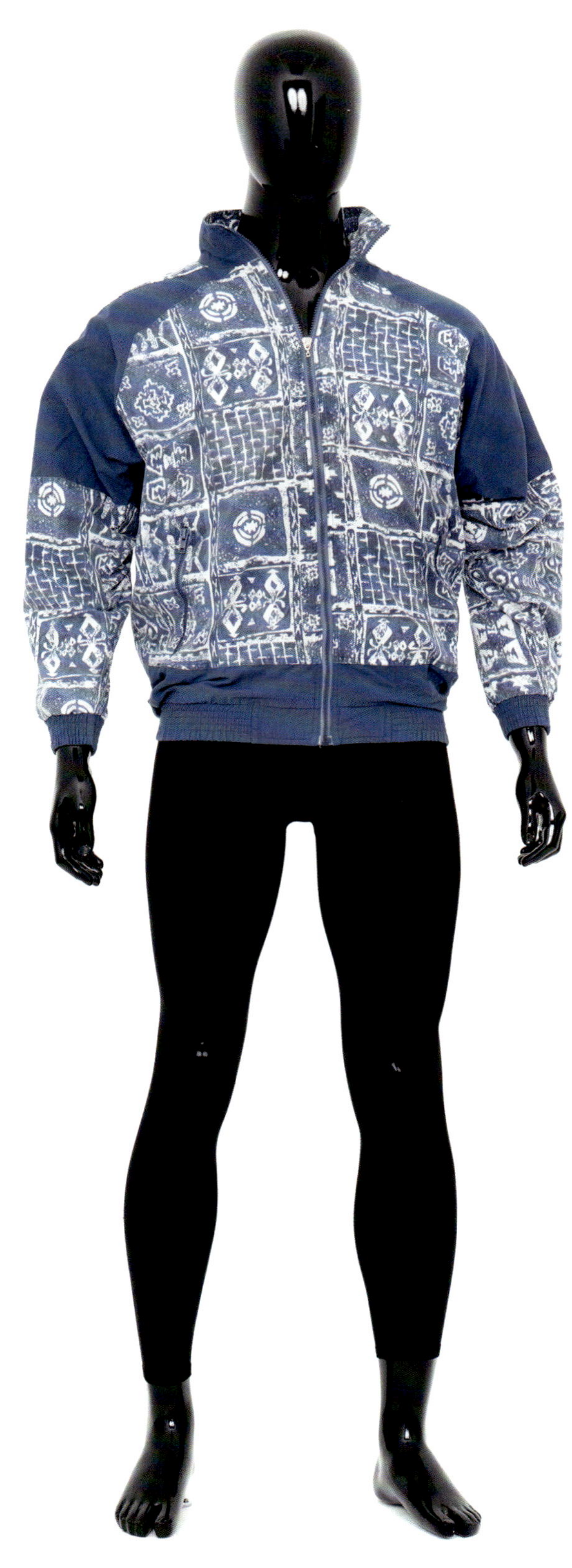

Cat. no. 30

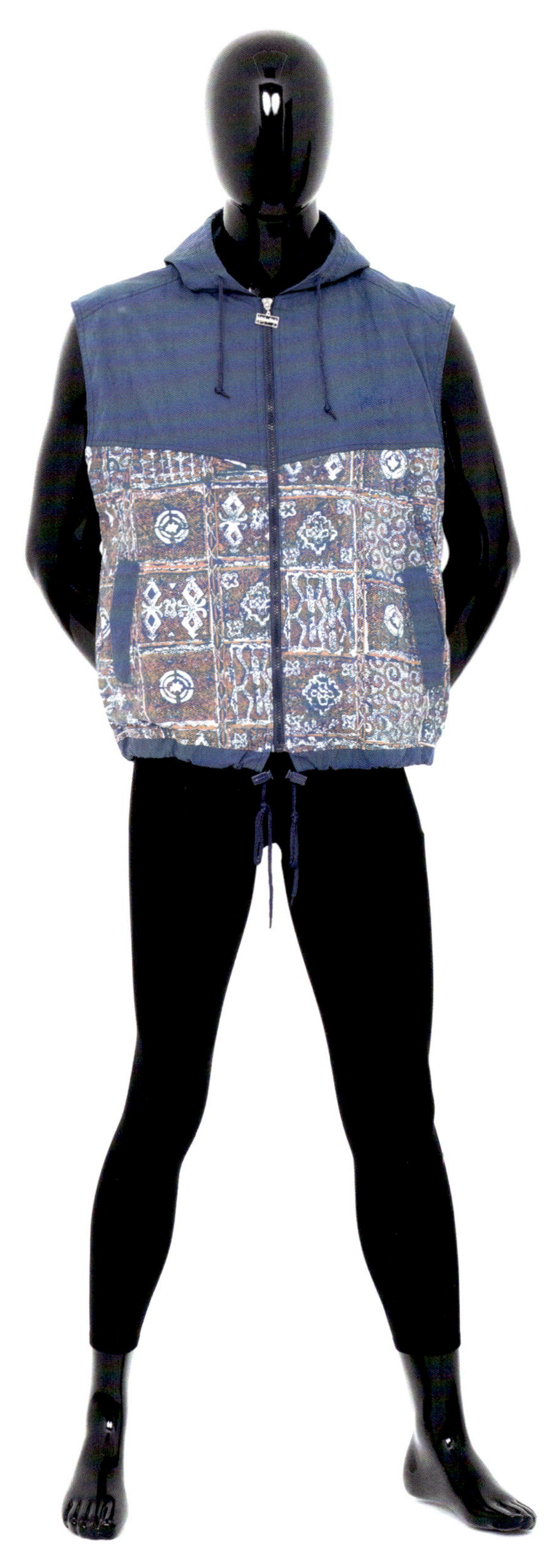

Cat. no. 31

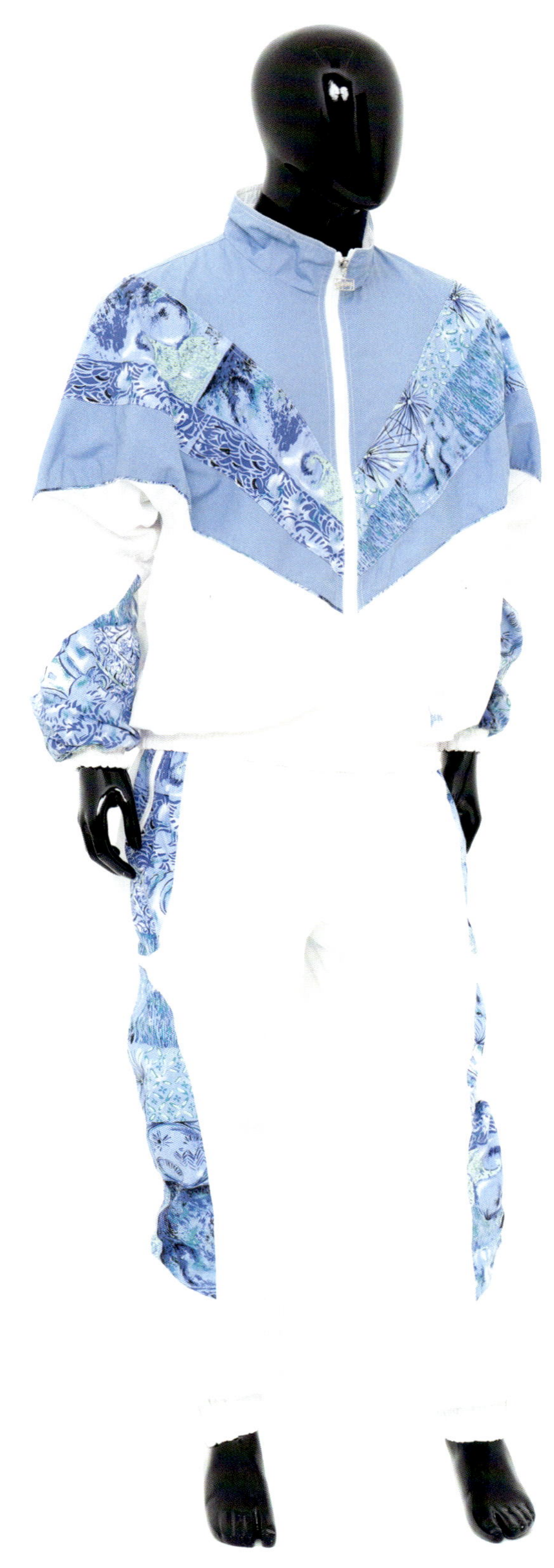

Cat. no. 32

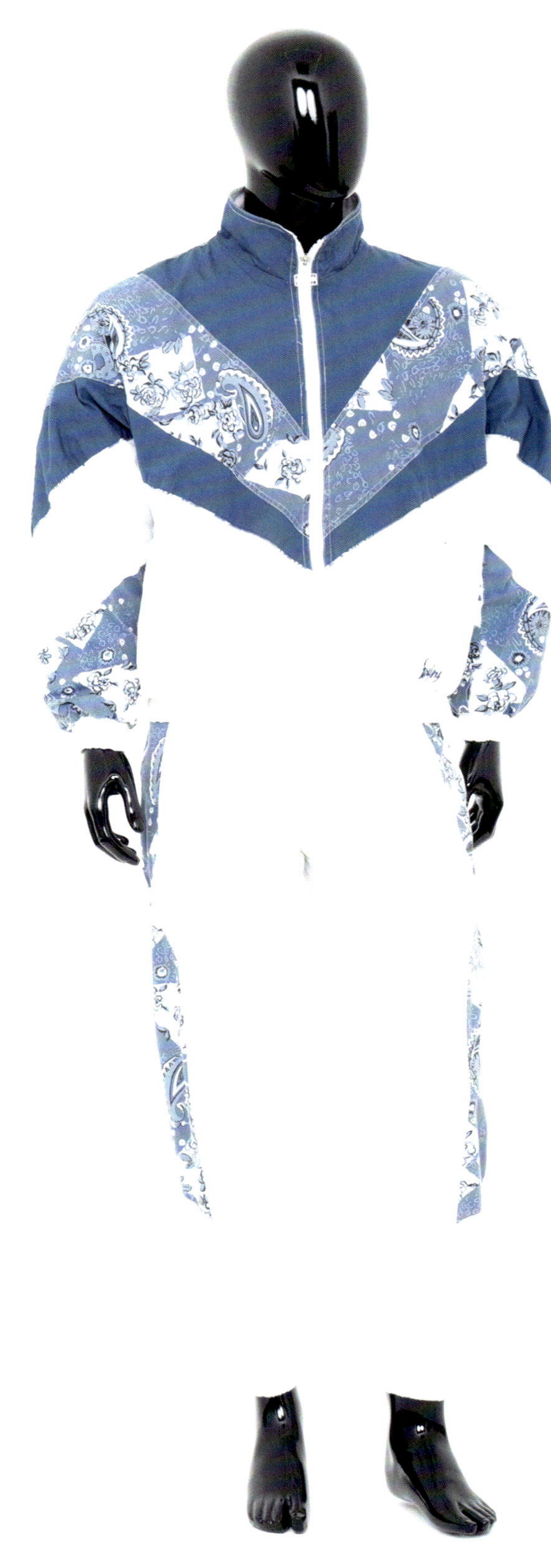

Cat. no. 33

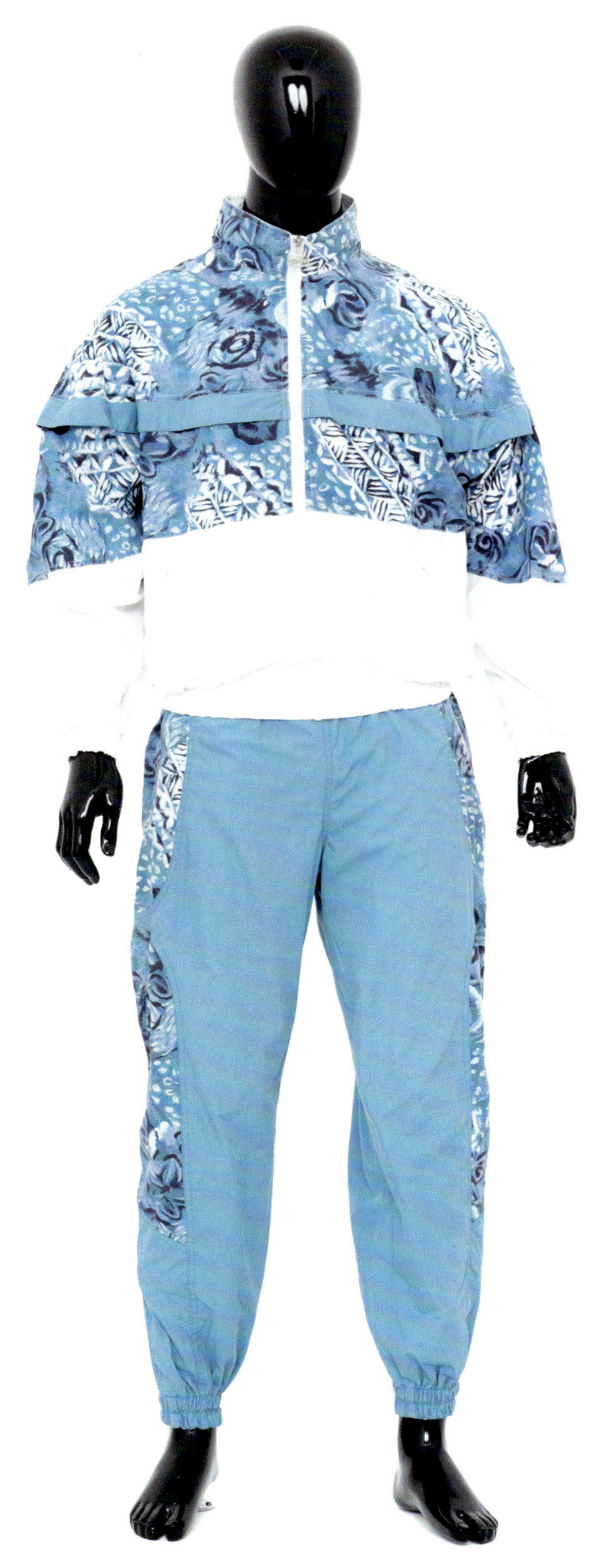

Cat. no. 34

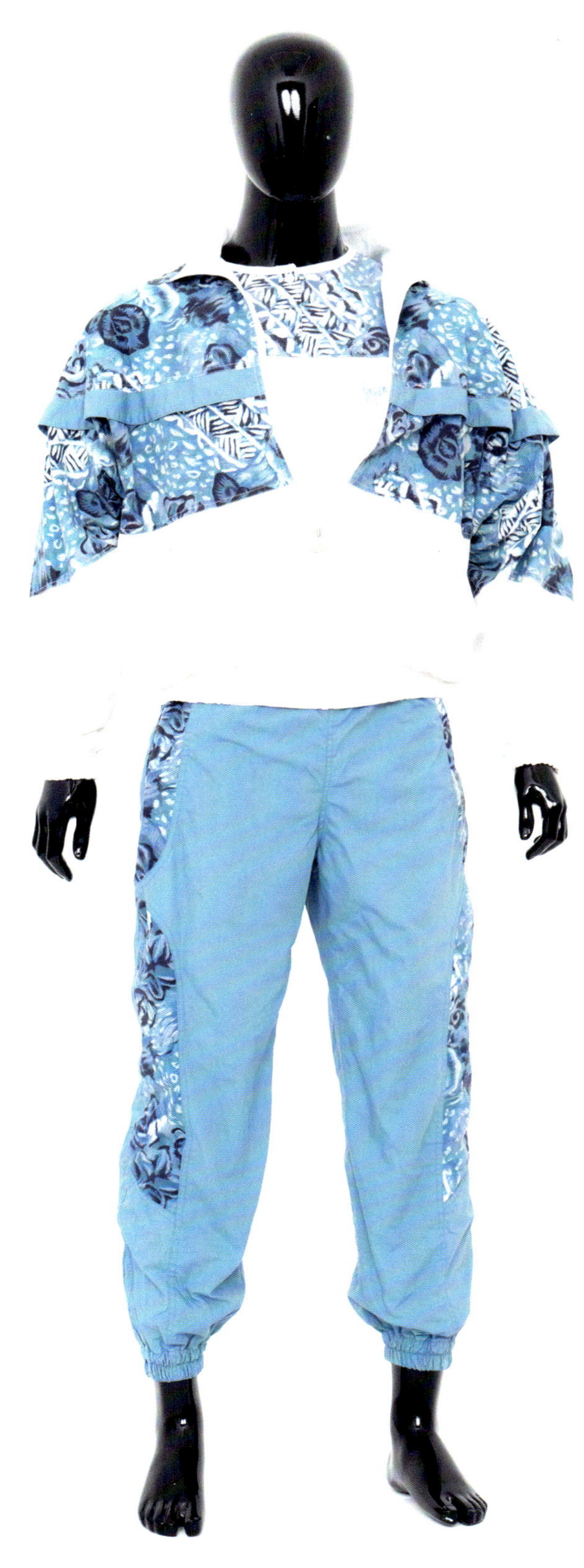

Cat. no. 35

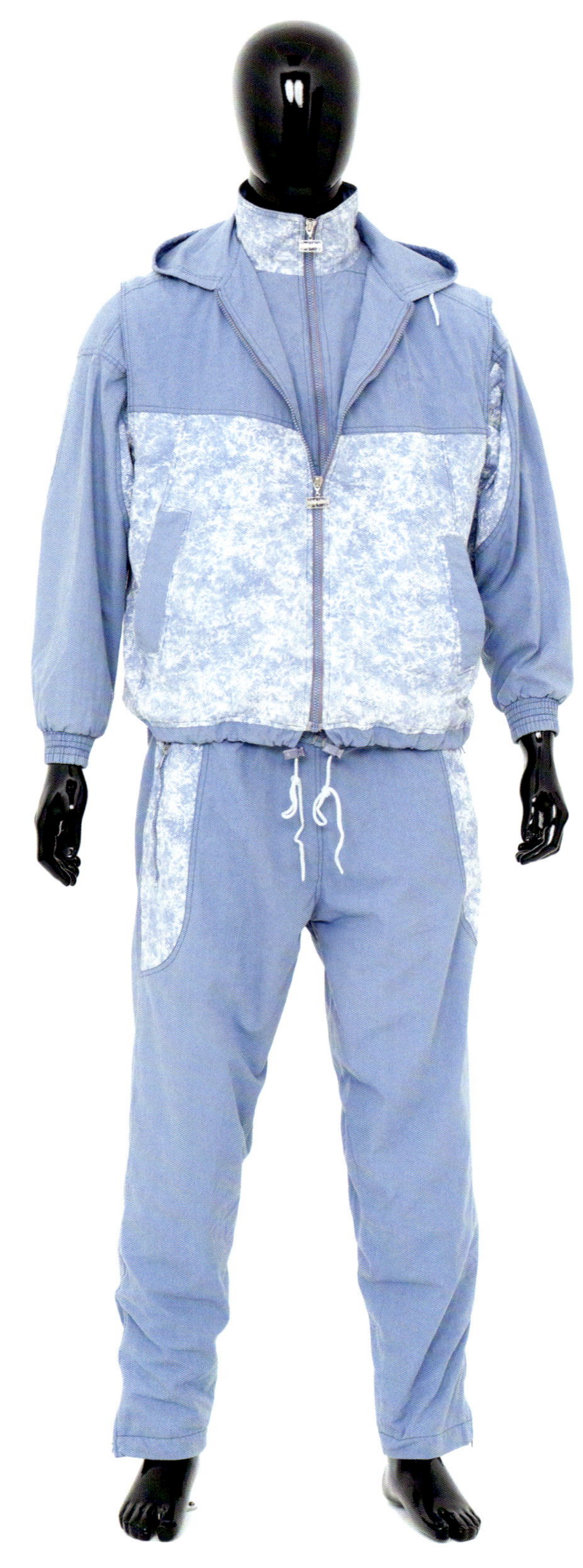

Cat. no. 36

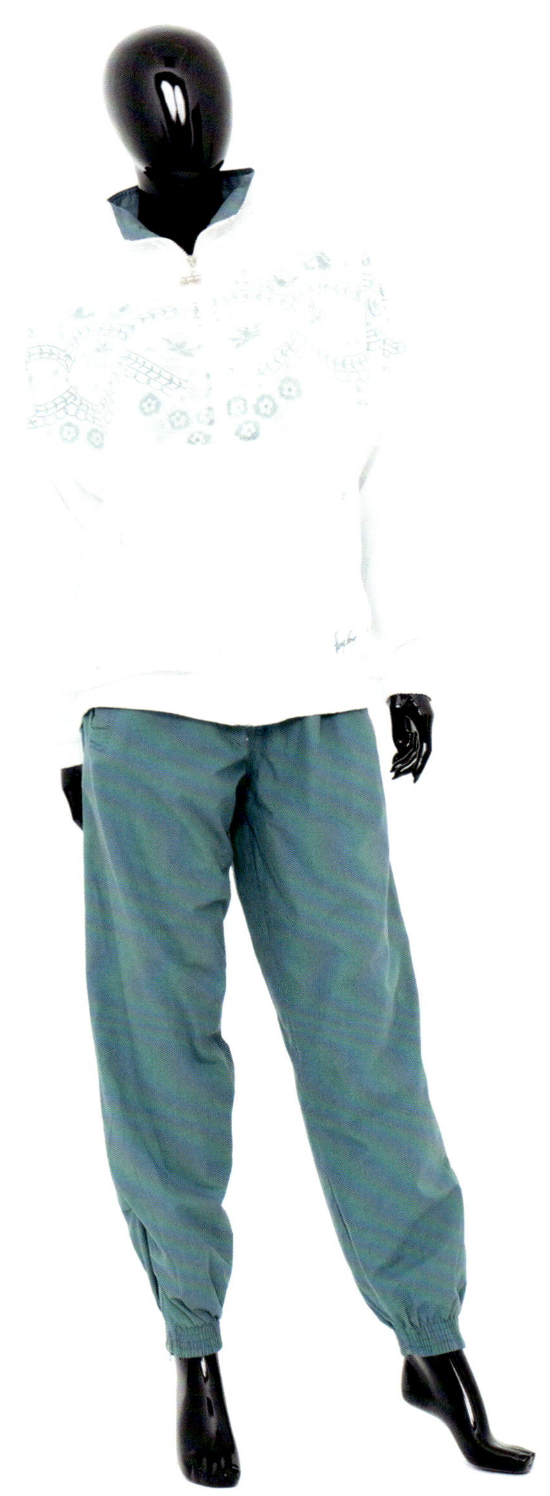

Cat. no. 37

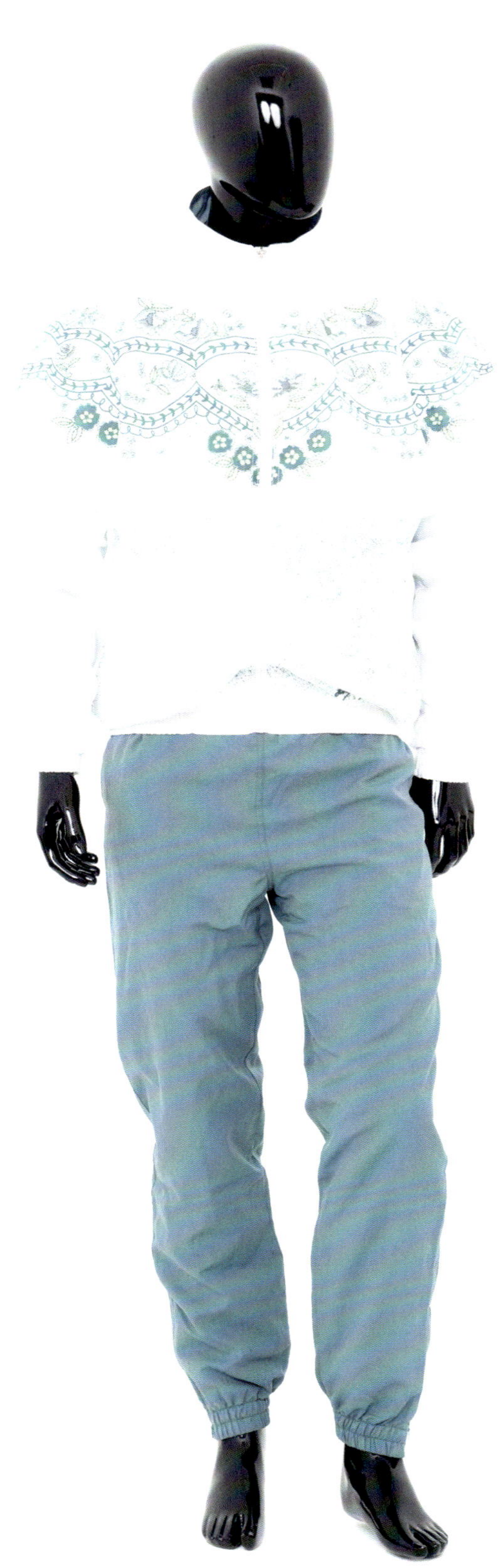

Cat. no. 38

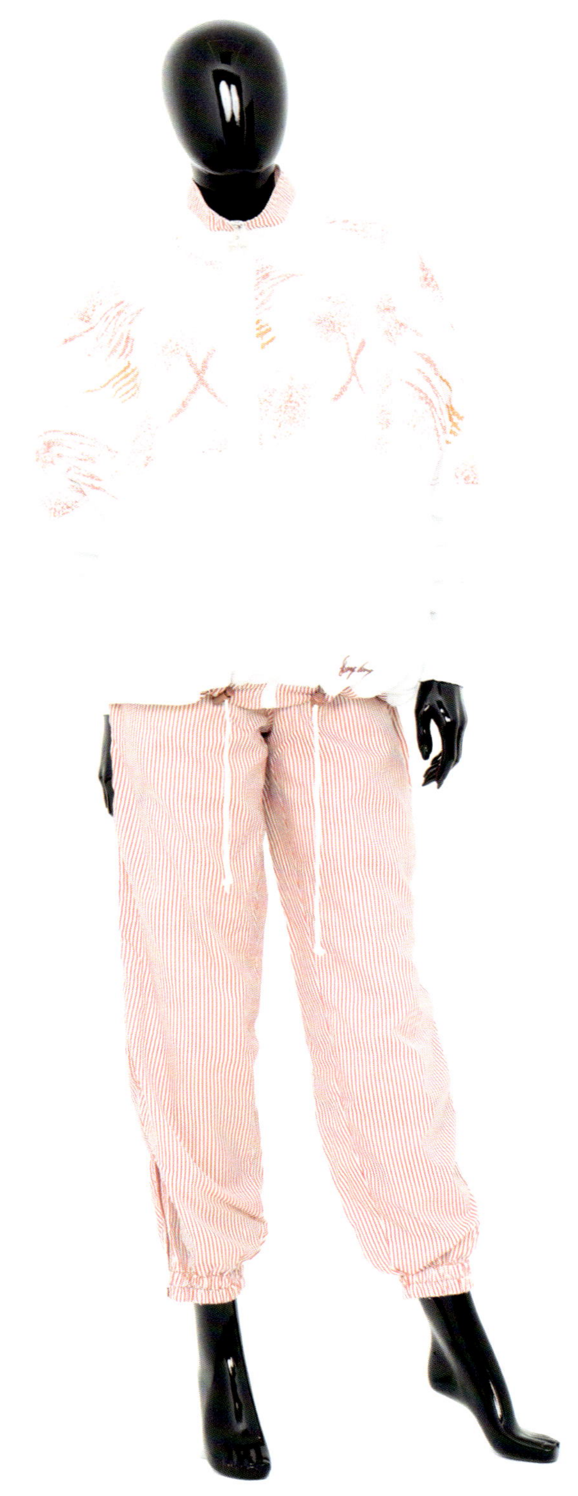

Cat. no. 39

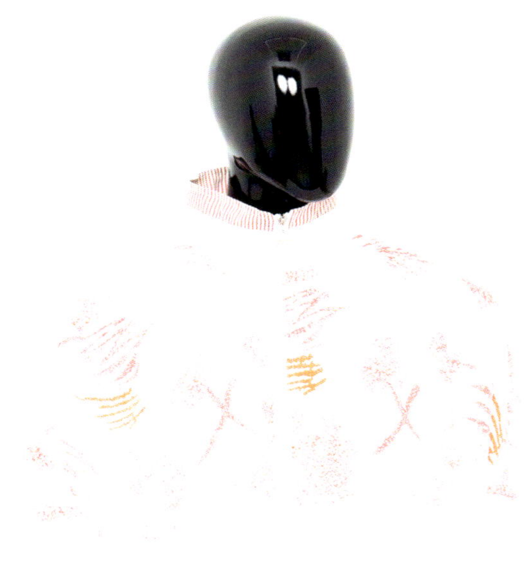

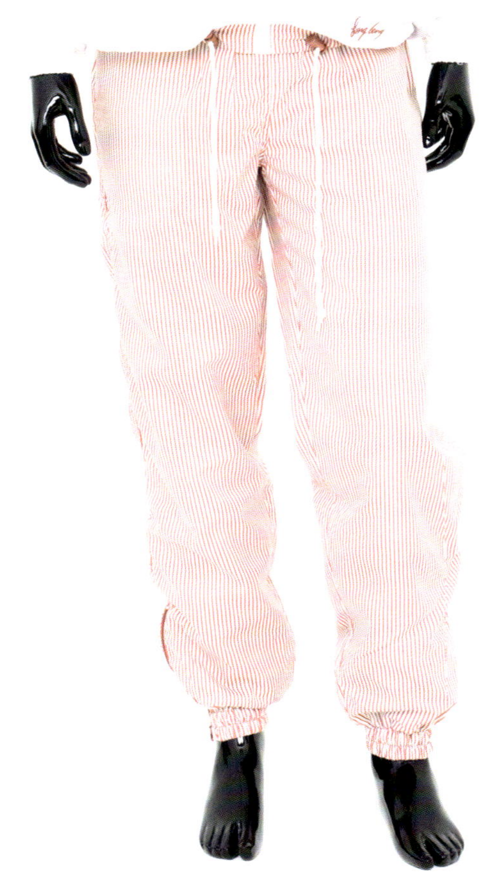

Cat. no. 40

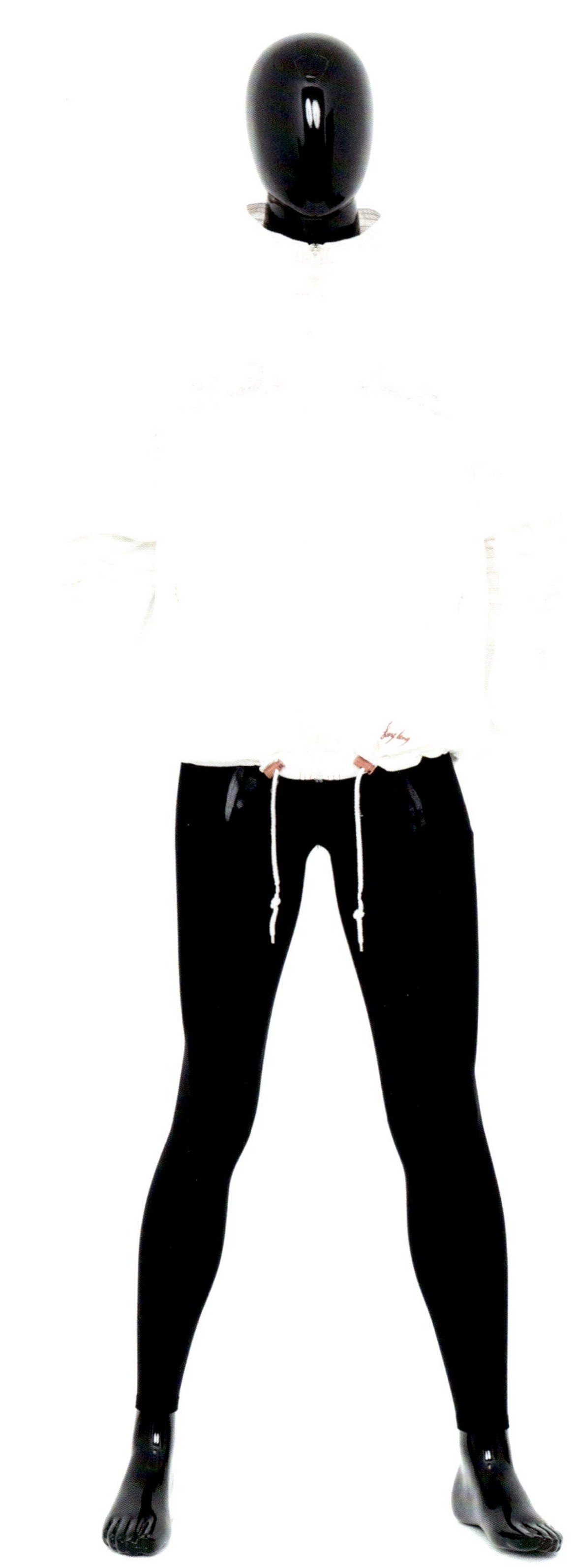

Cat. no. 41

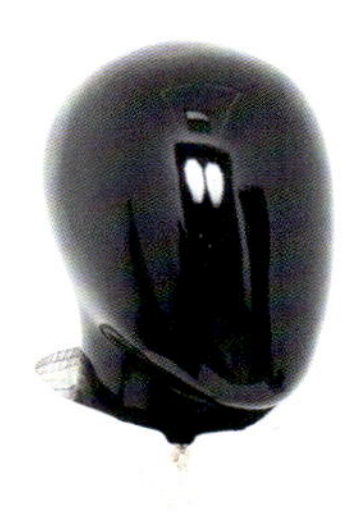
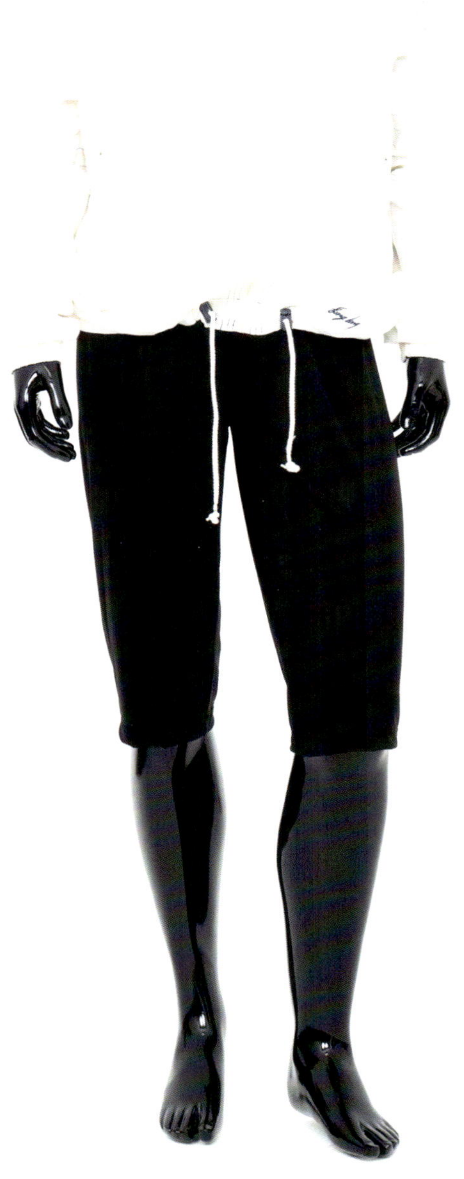

Cat. no. 42

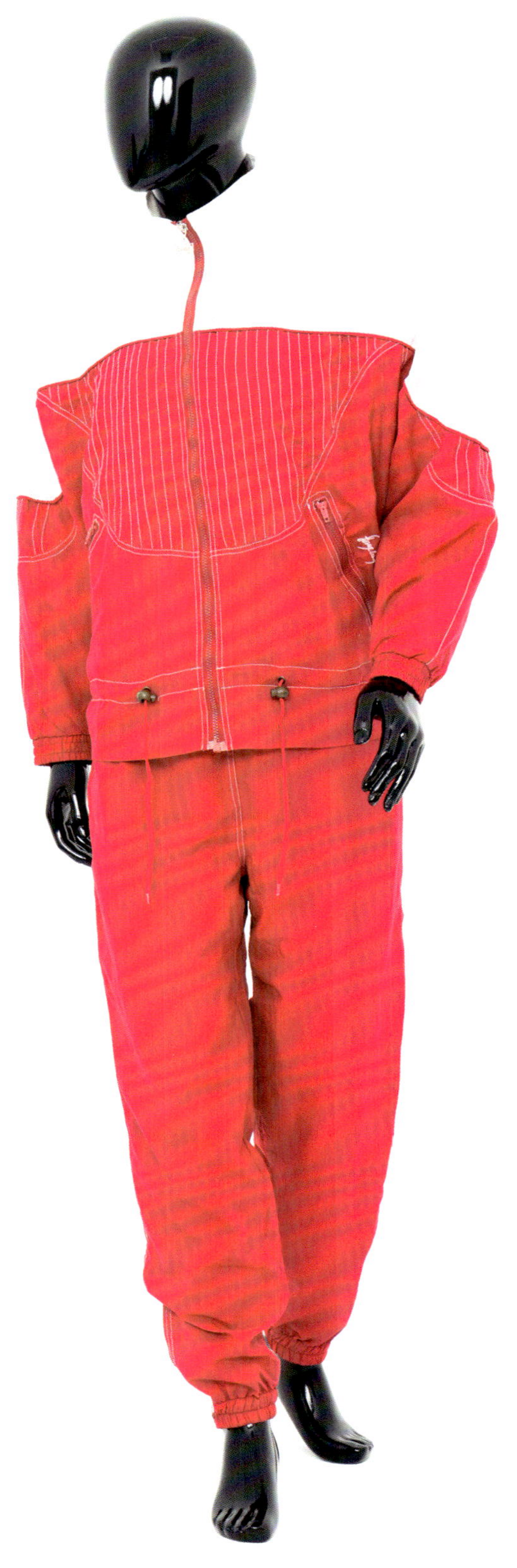

Cat. no. 43

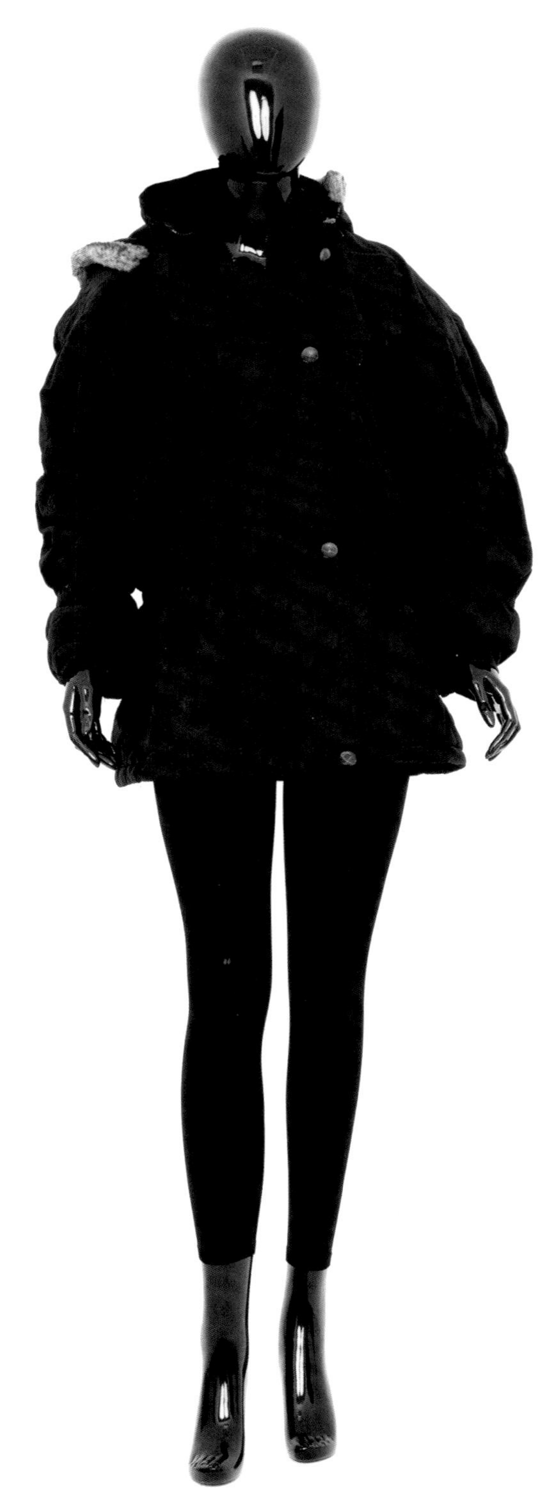

Cat. no. 44

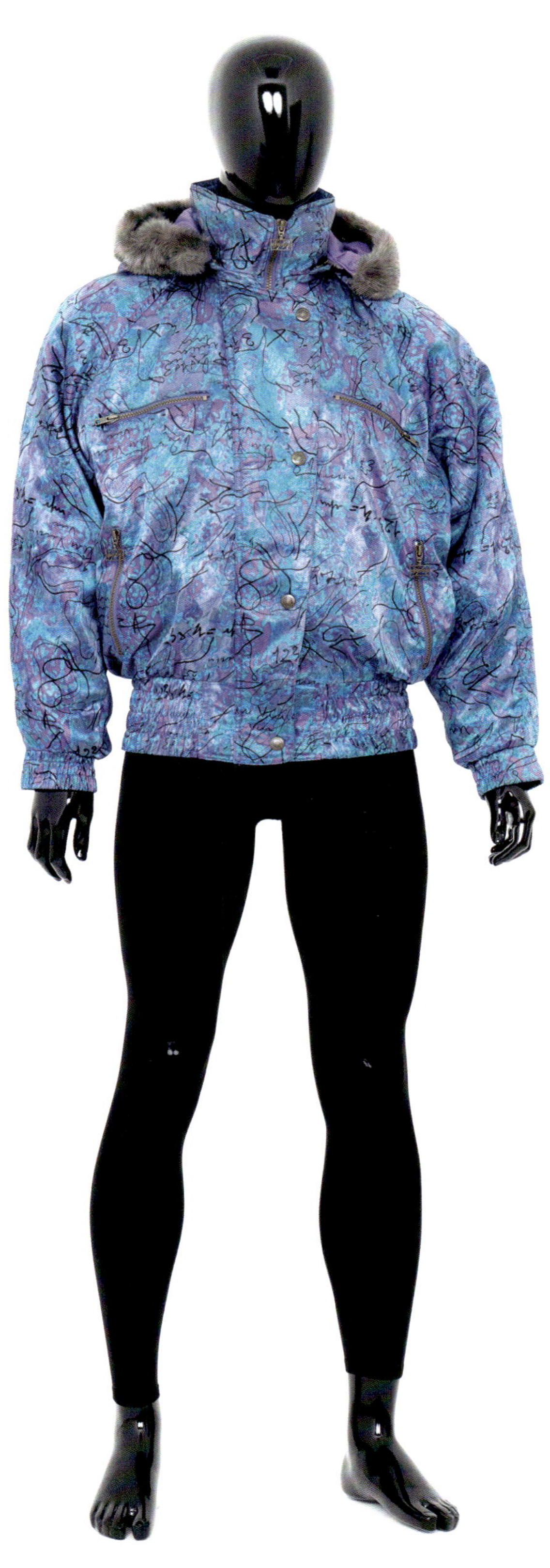

Cat. no. 45

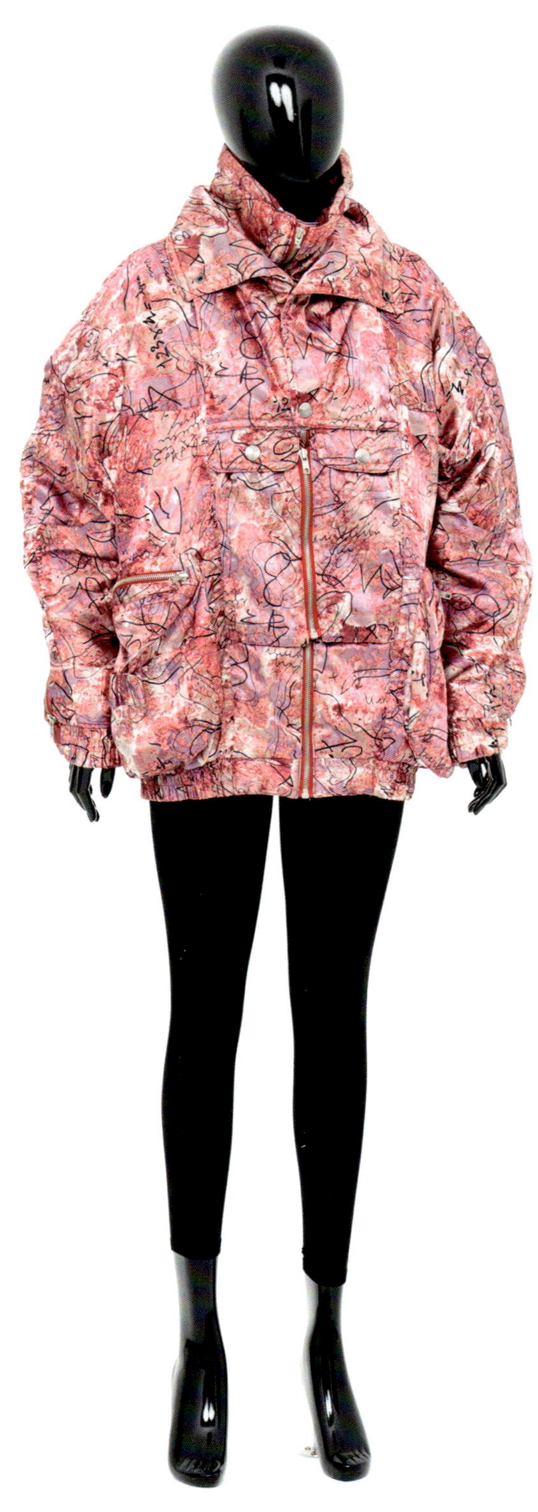

Cat. no. 46

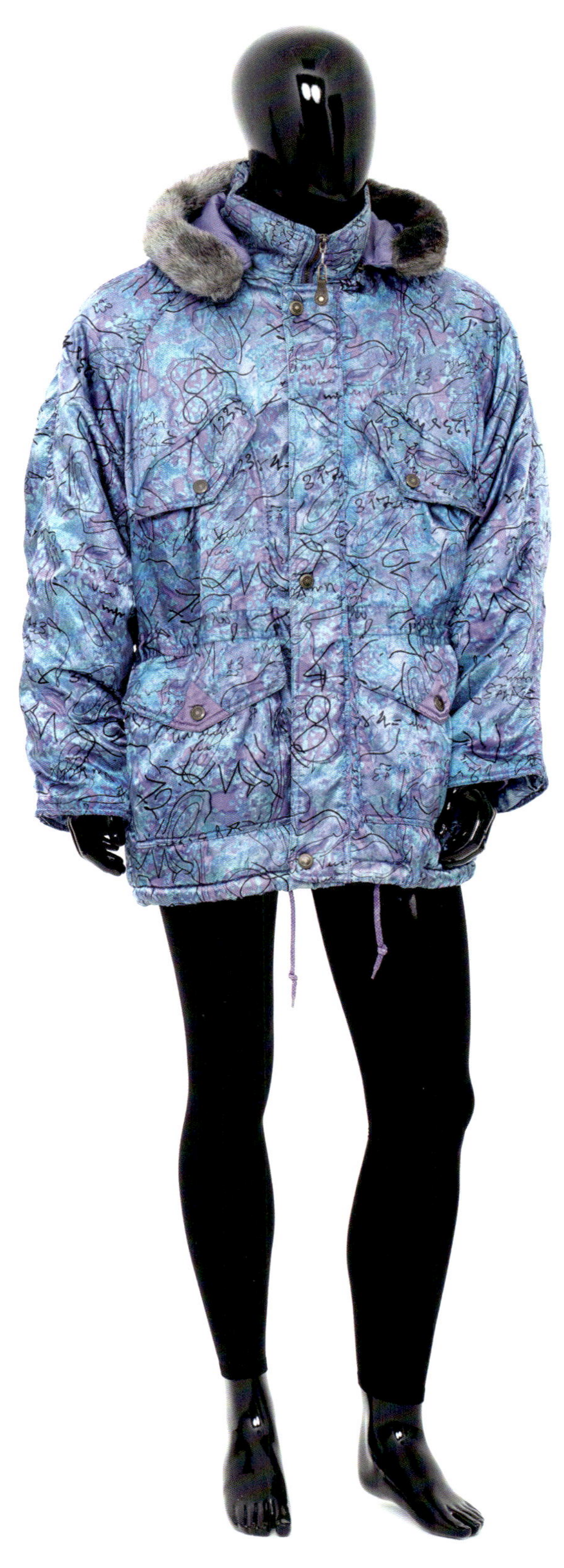

Cat. no. 47

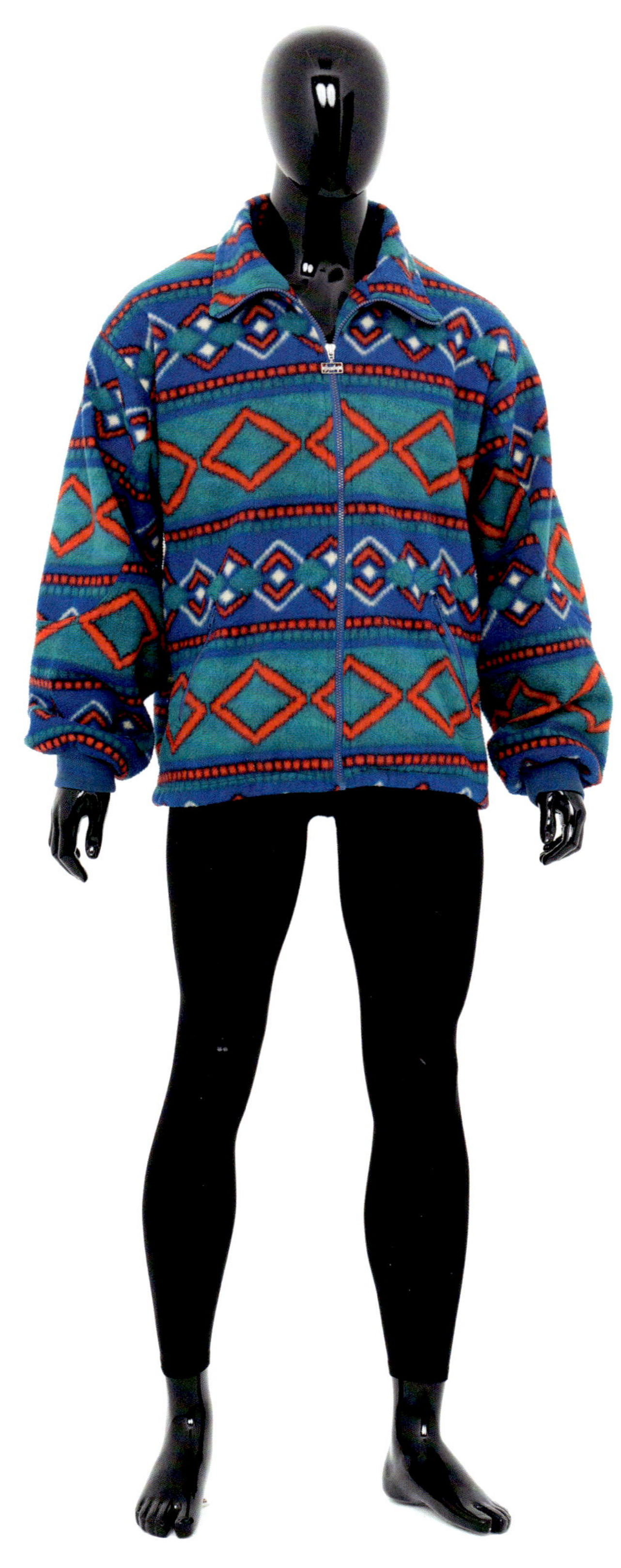

Cat. no. 48

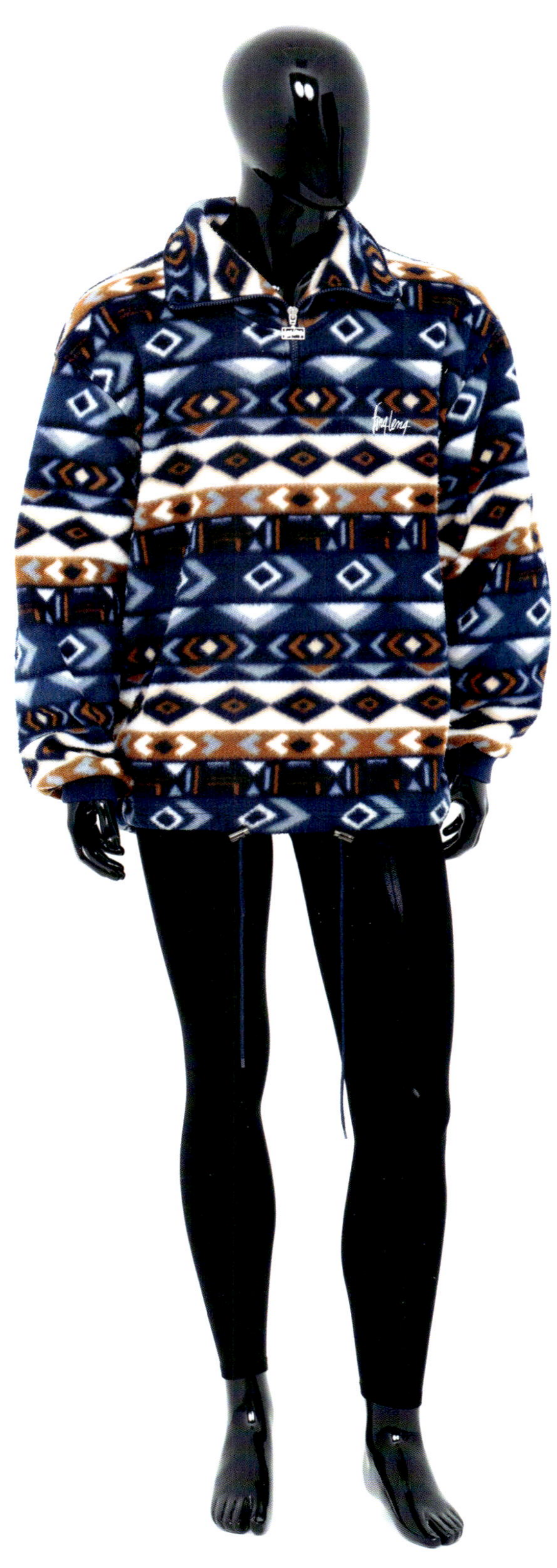

Cat. no. 49

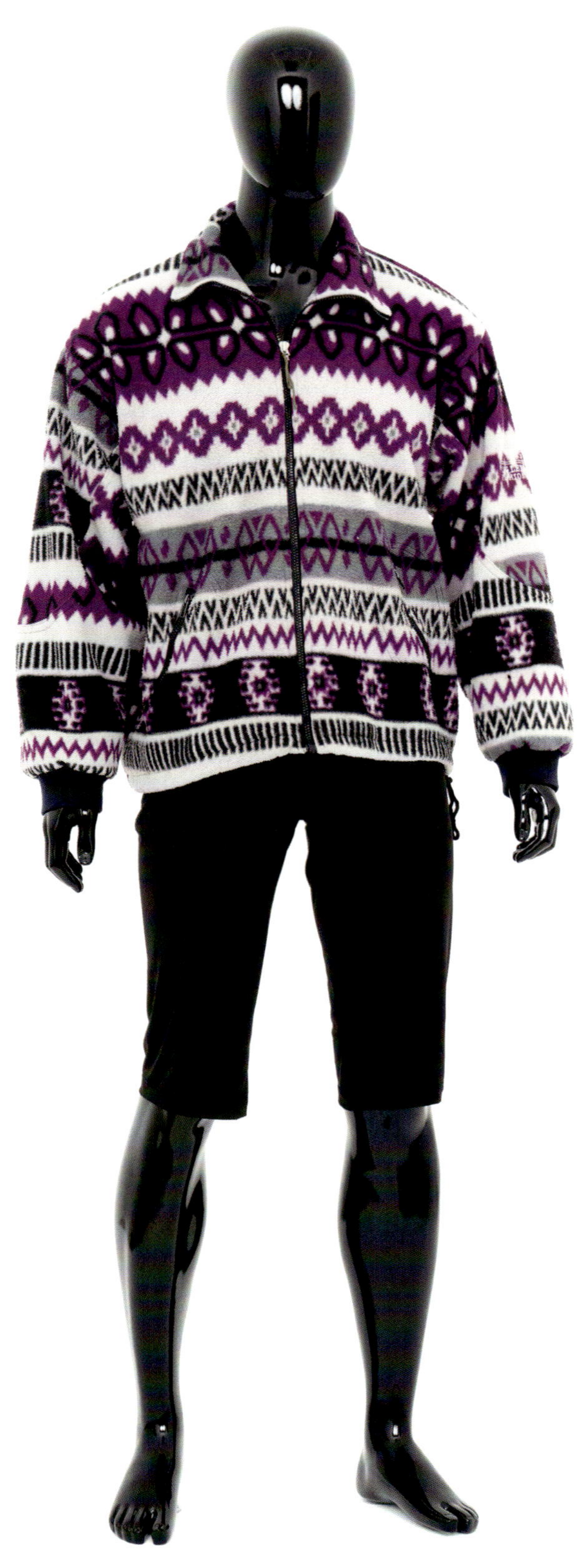

Cat. no. 50

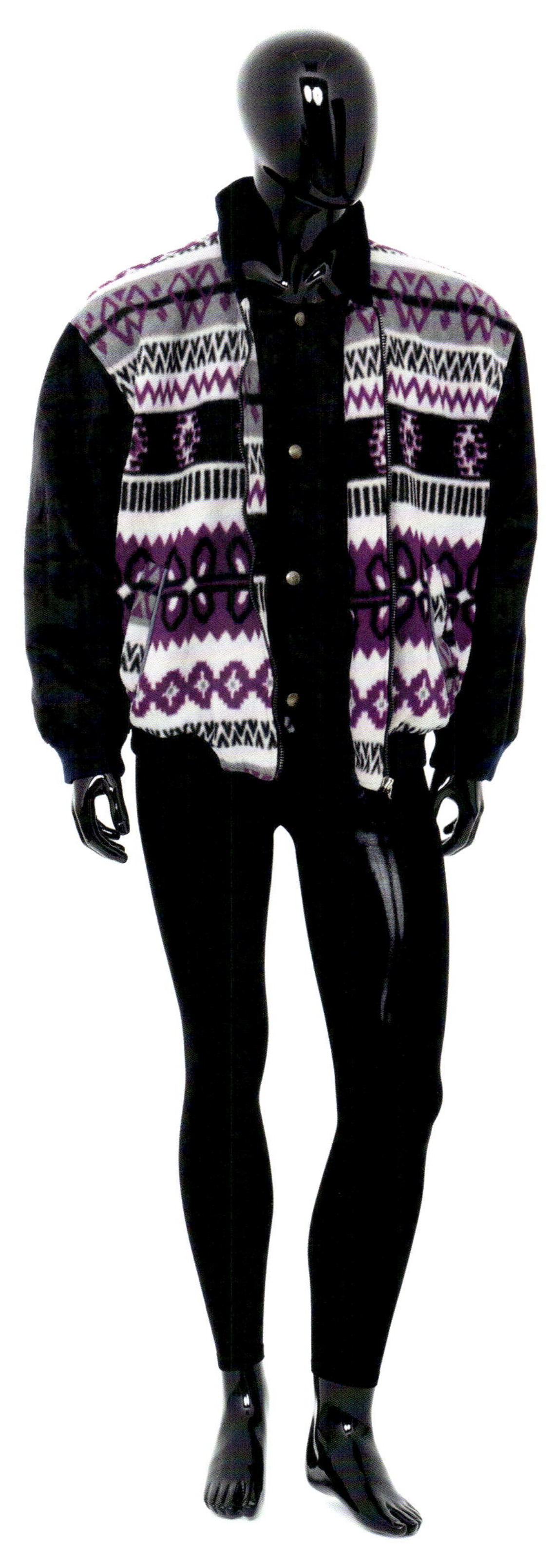

Cat. no. 51

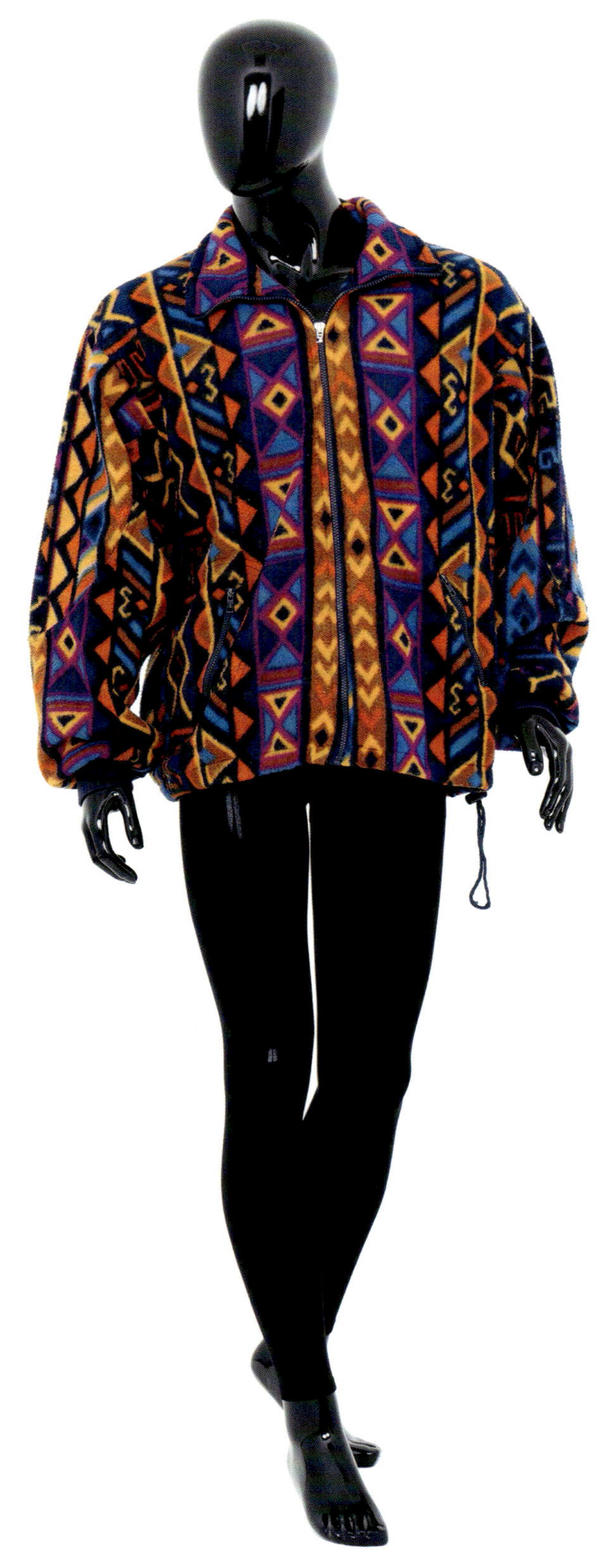

Cat. no. 52

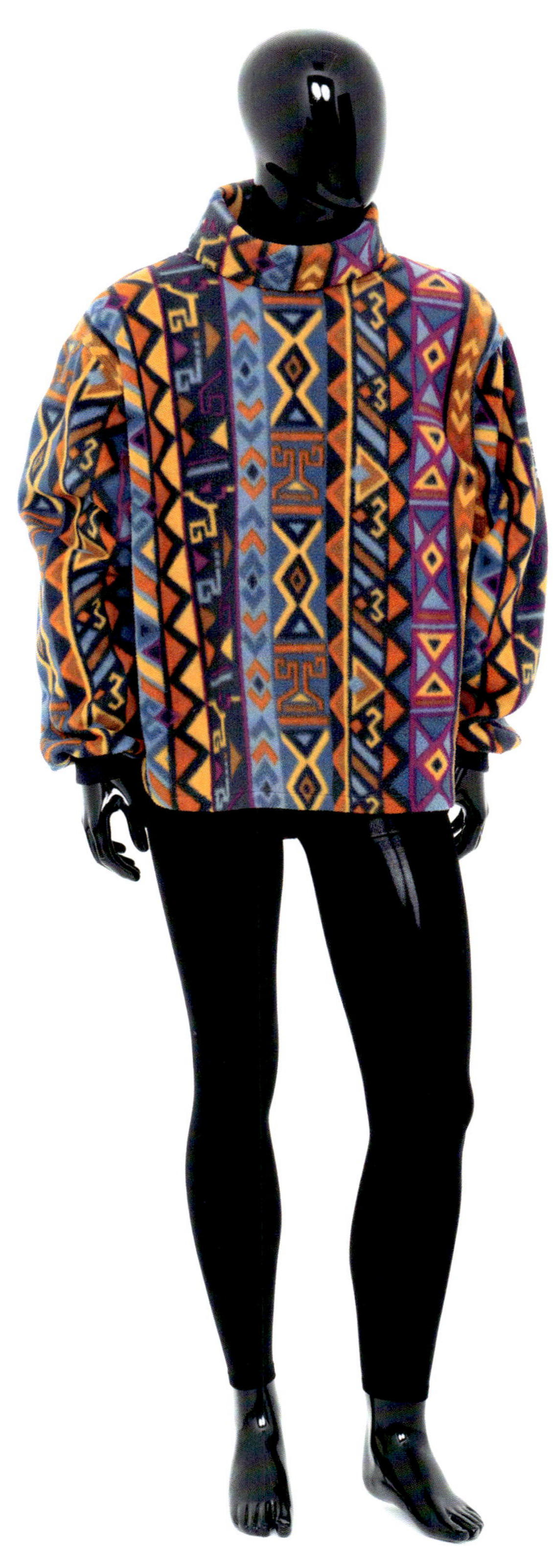

Cat. no. 53

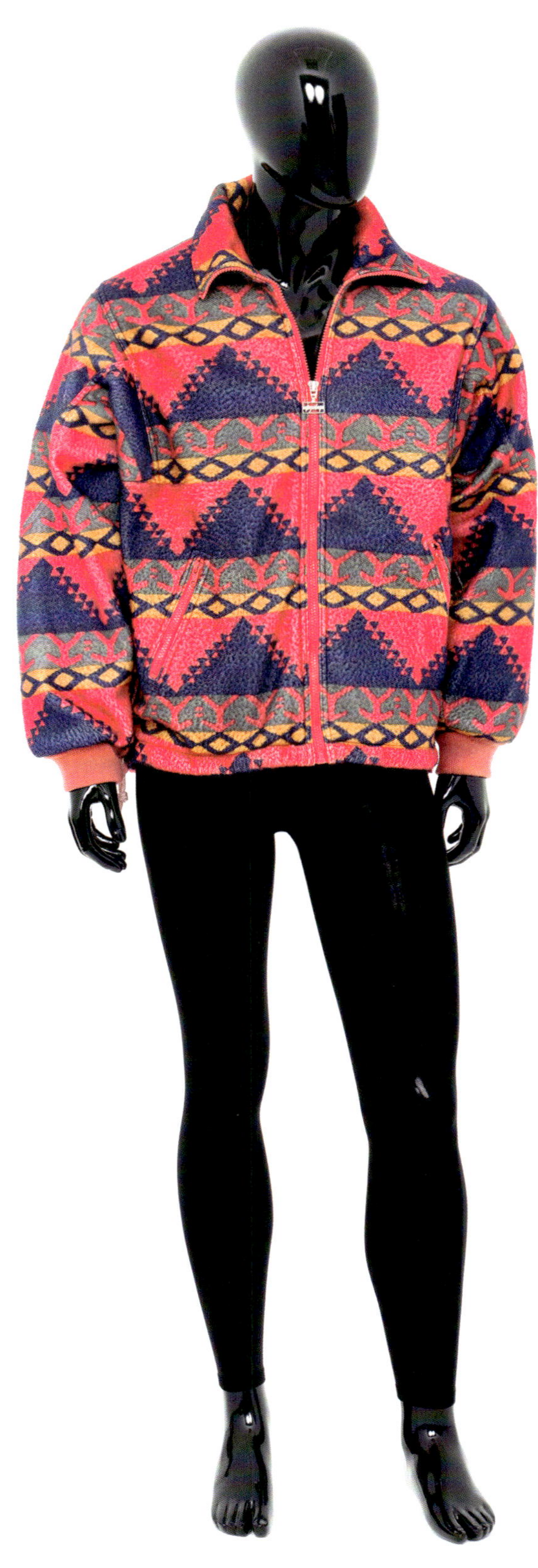

Cat. no. 54

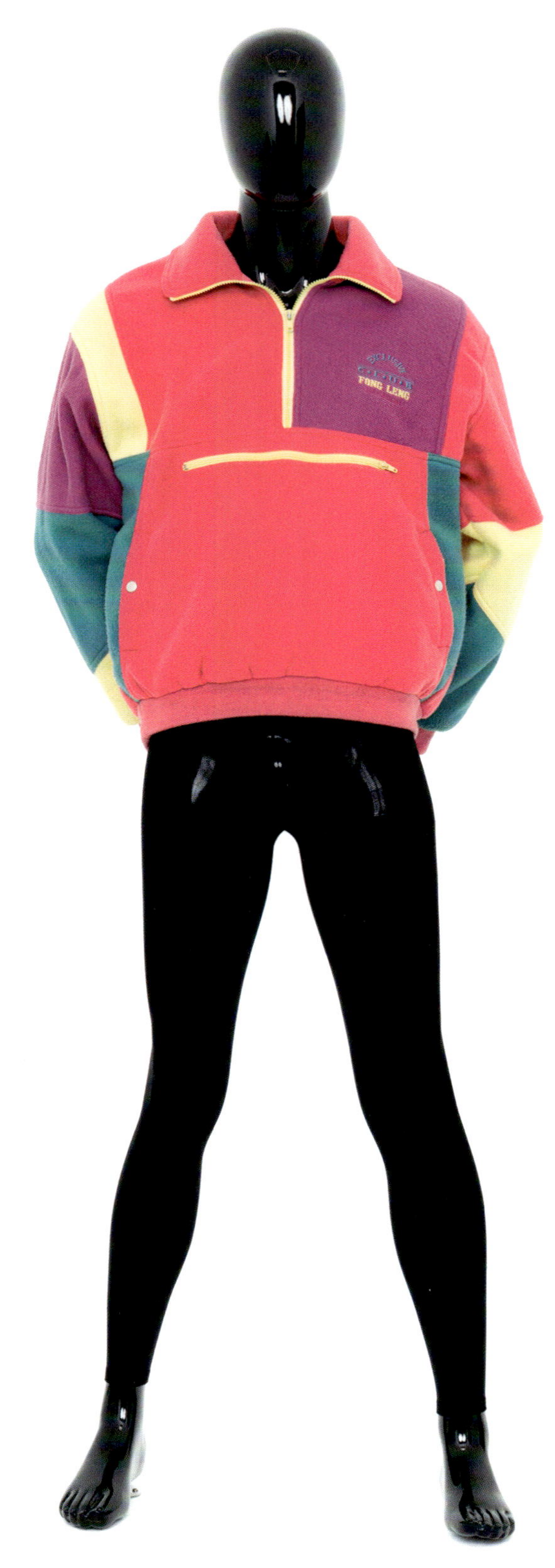

Cat. no. 55

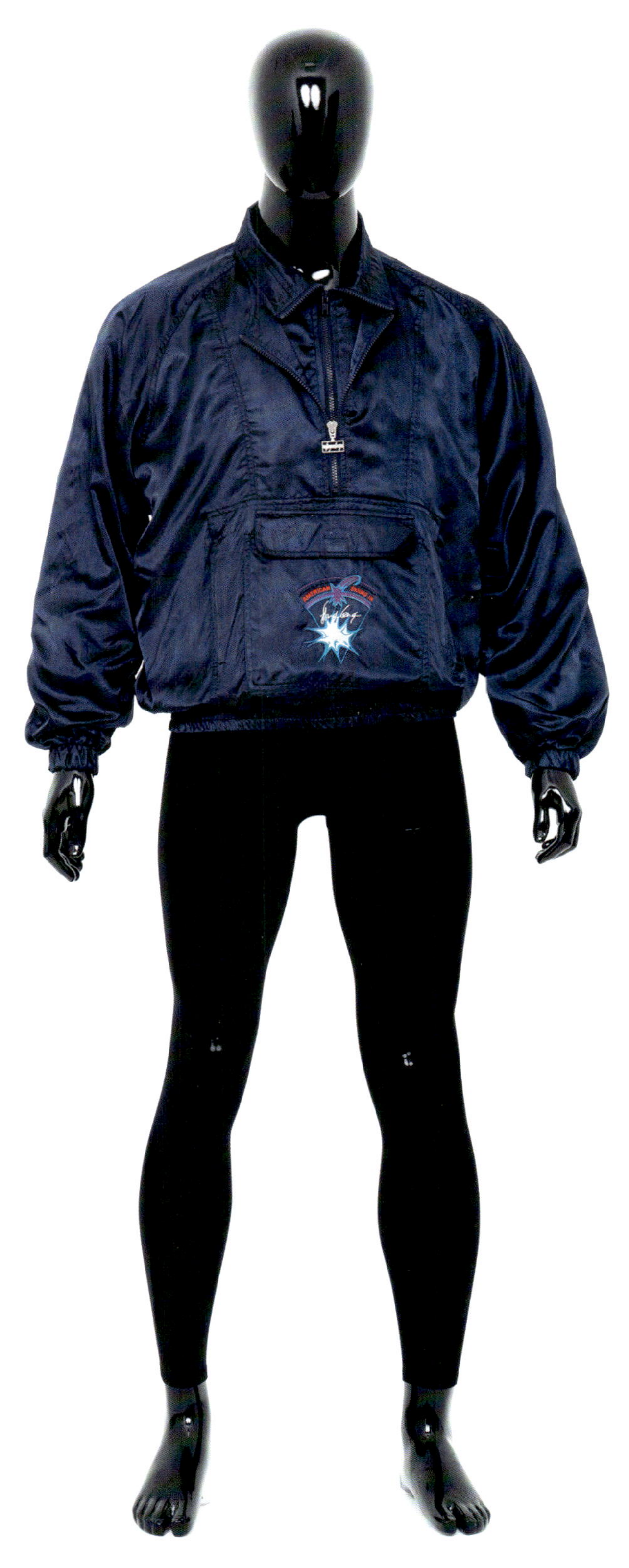

Cat. no. 56

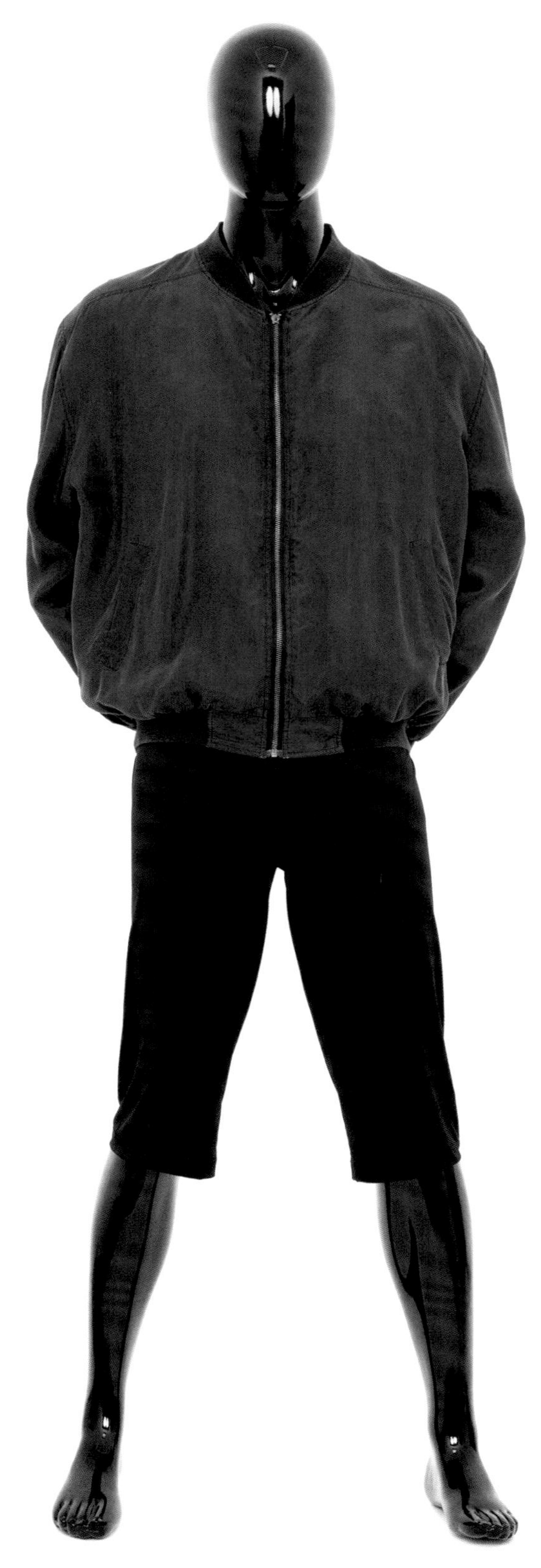

Cat. no. 57

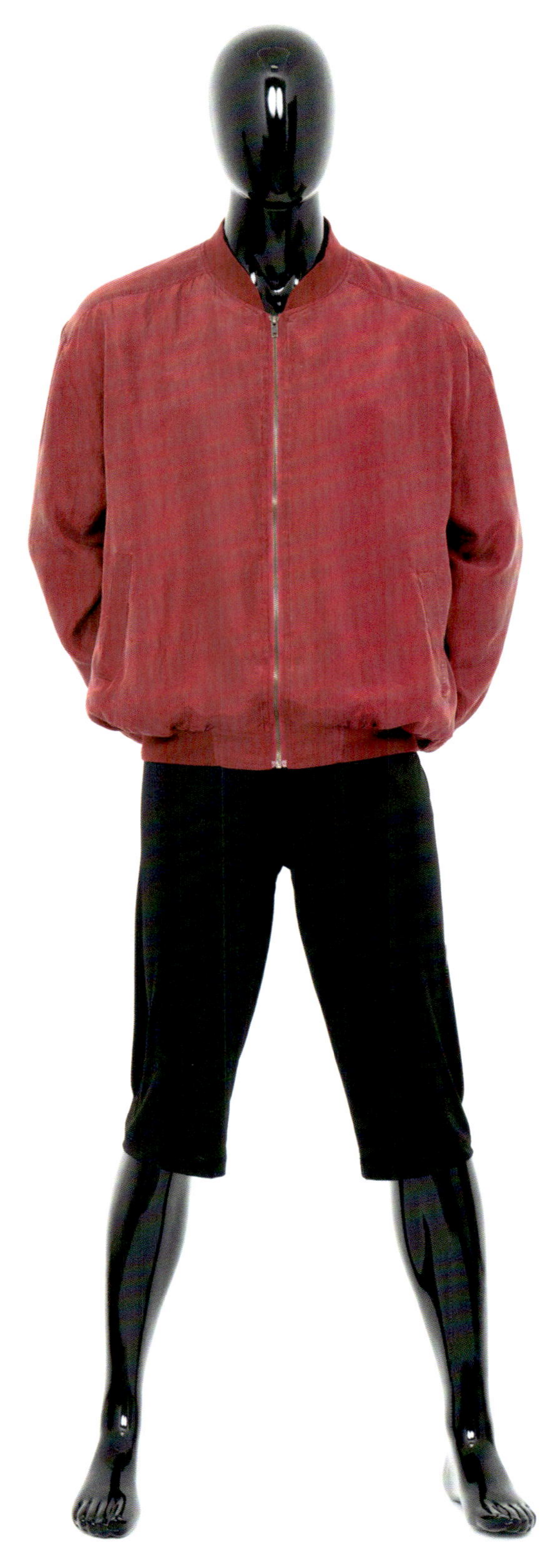

Cat. no. 58

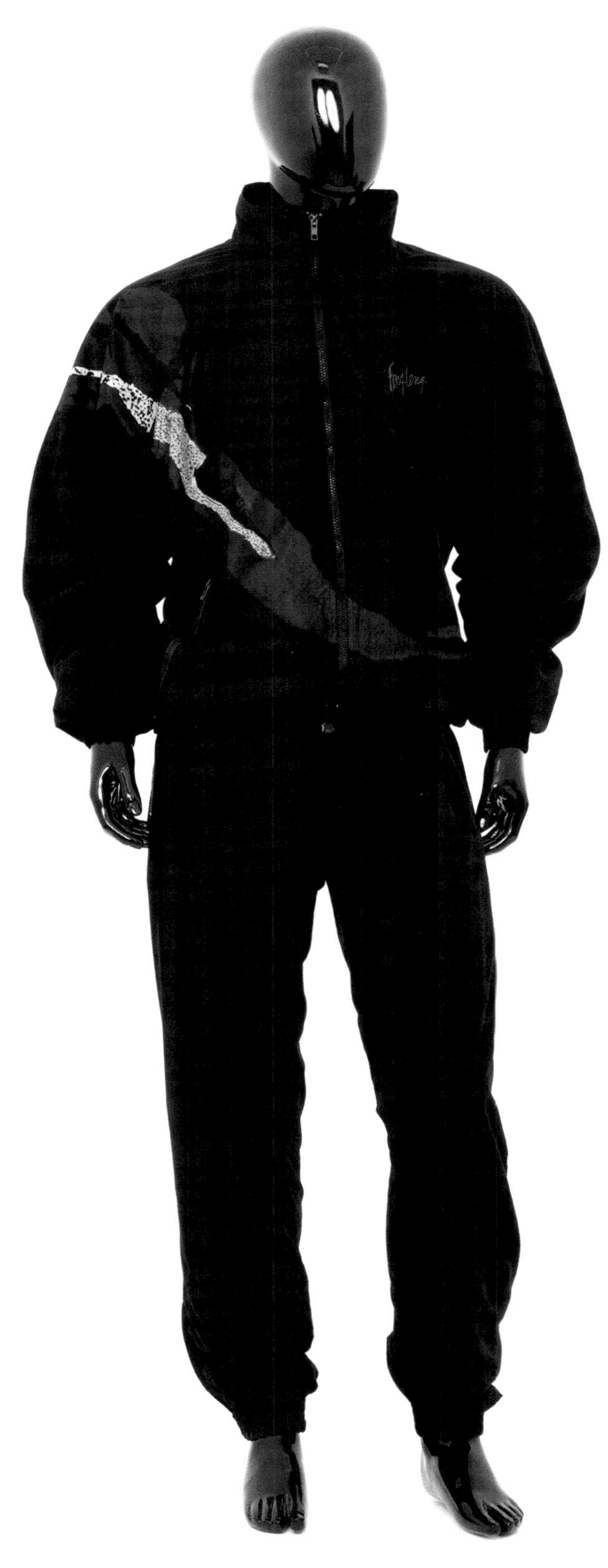

Cat. no. 59

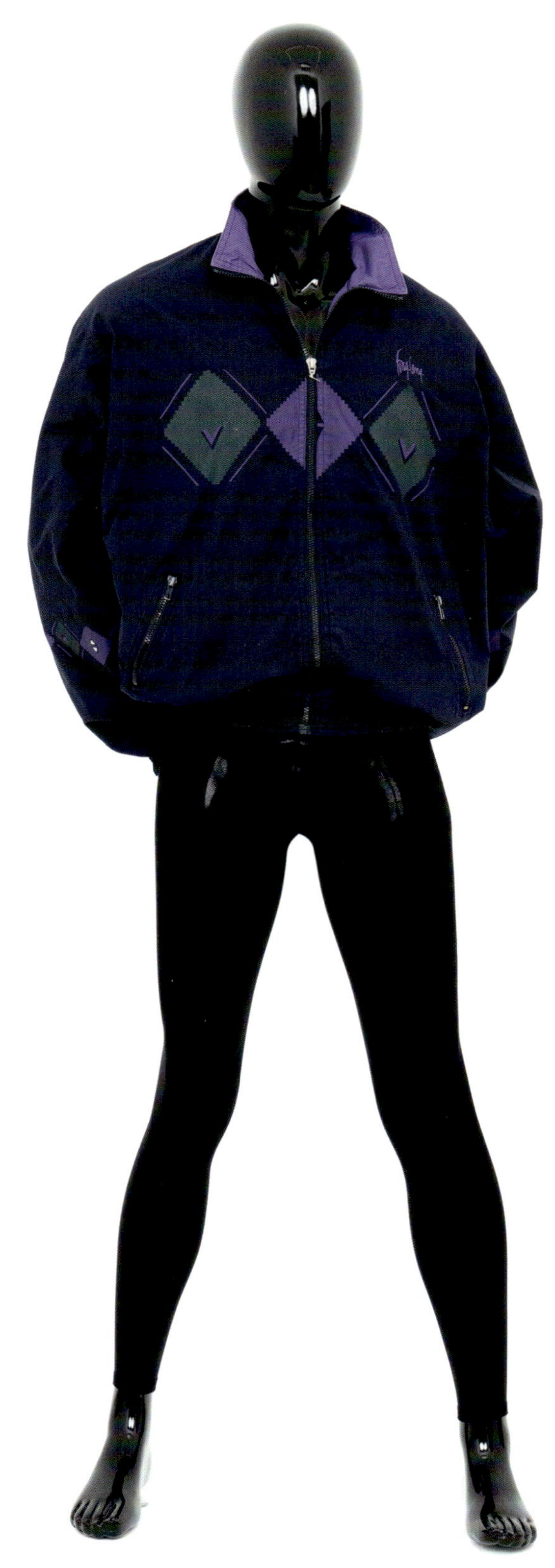

Cat. no. 60

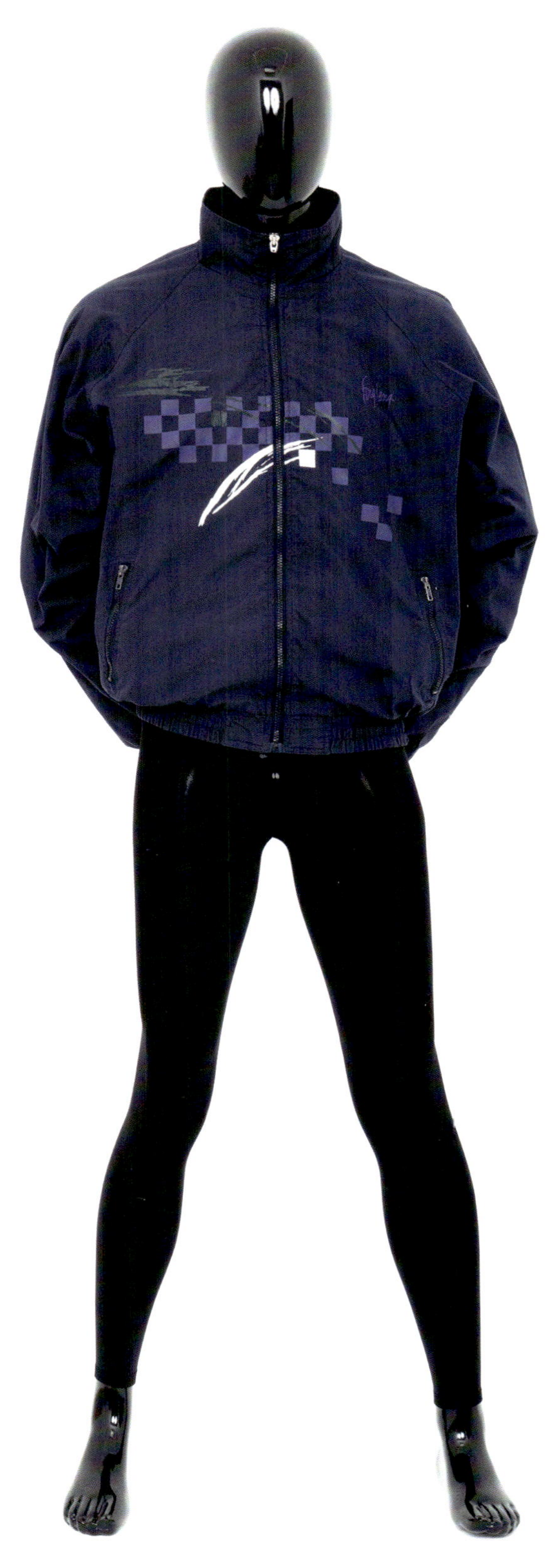

Cat. no. 61

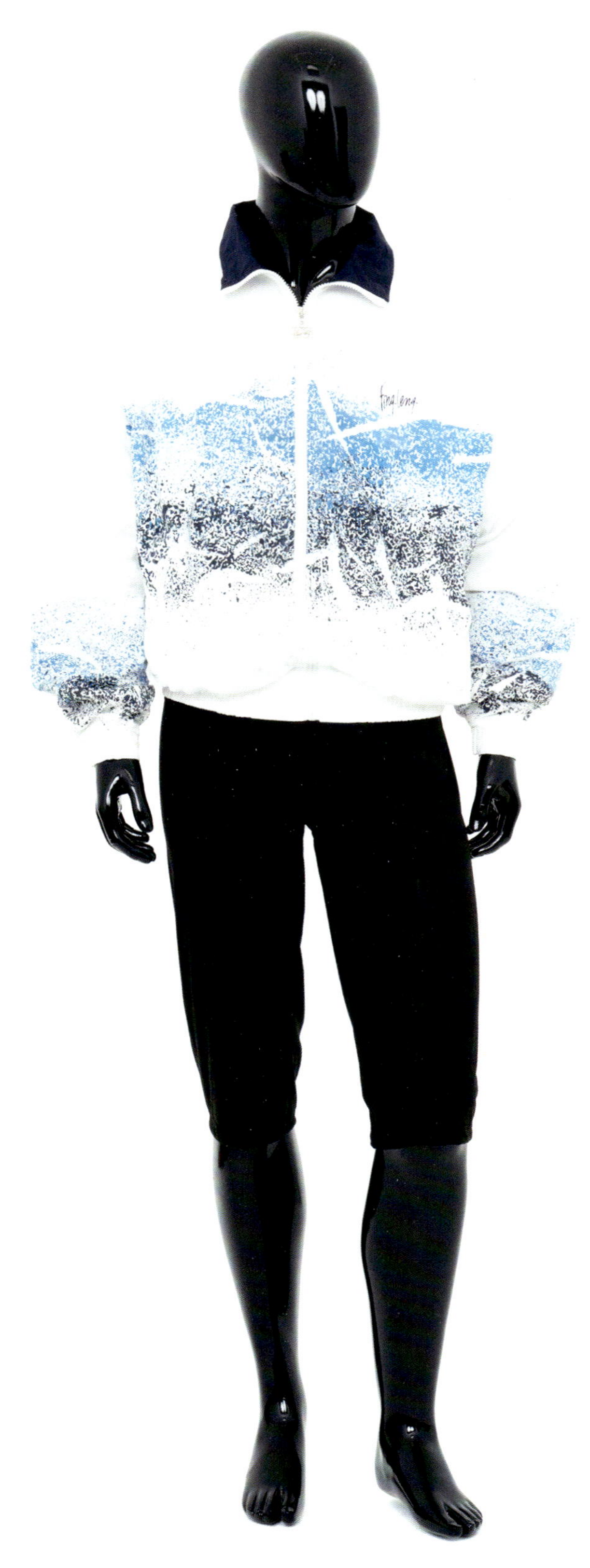

Cat. no. 62

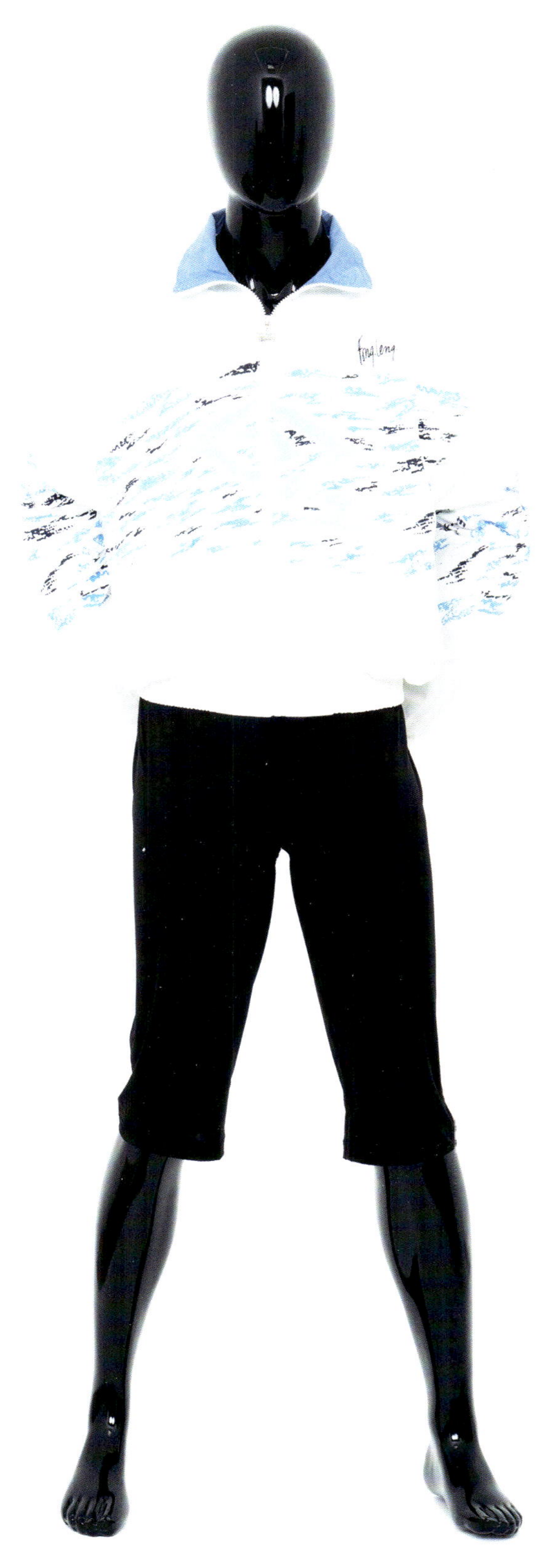

Cat. no. 63

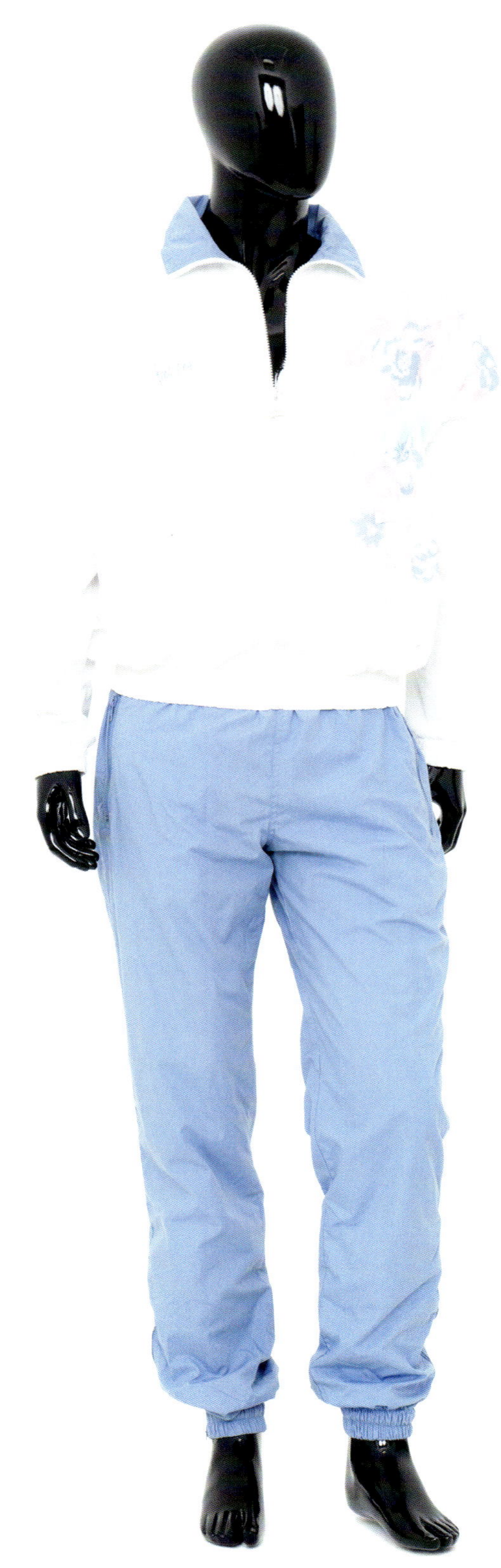

Cat. no. 64

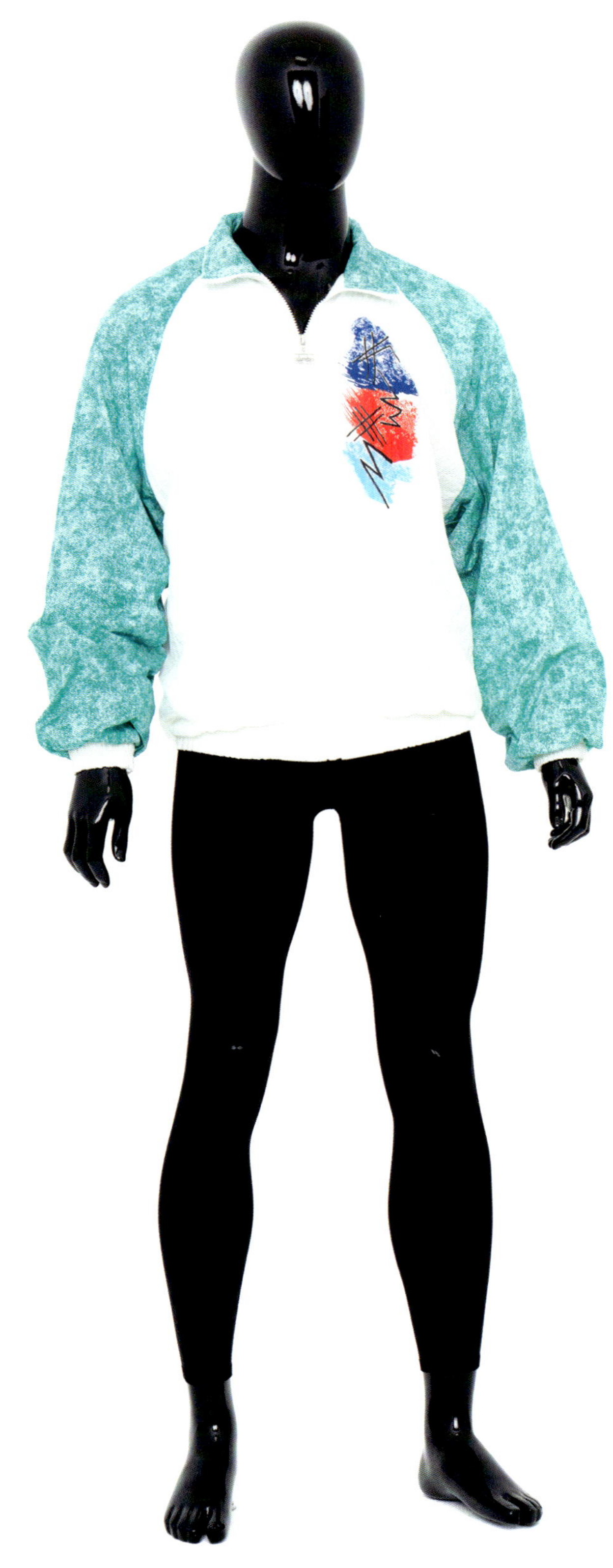

Cat. no. 65

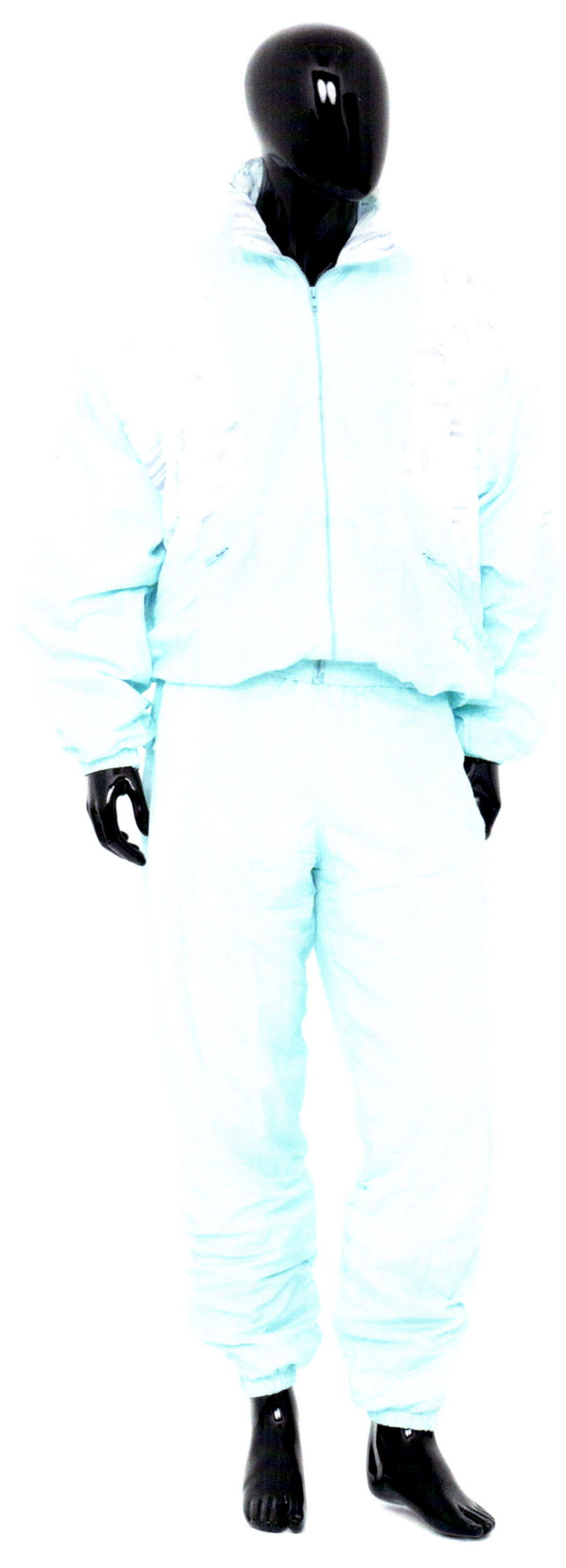

Cat. no. 66

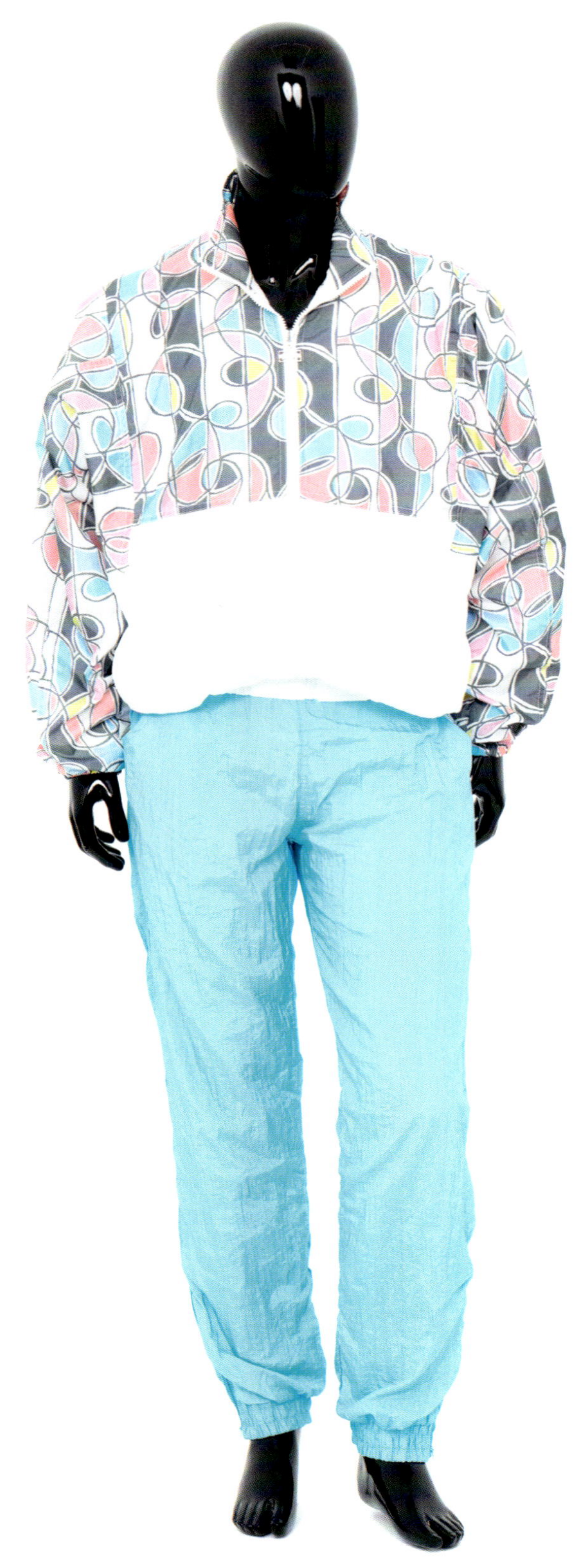

Cat. no. 67

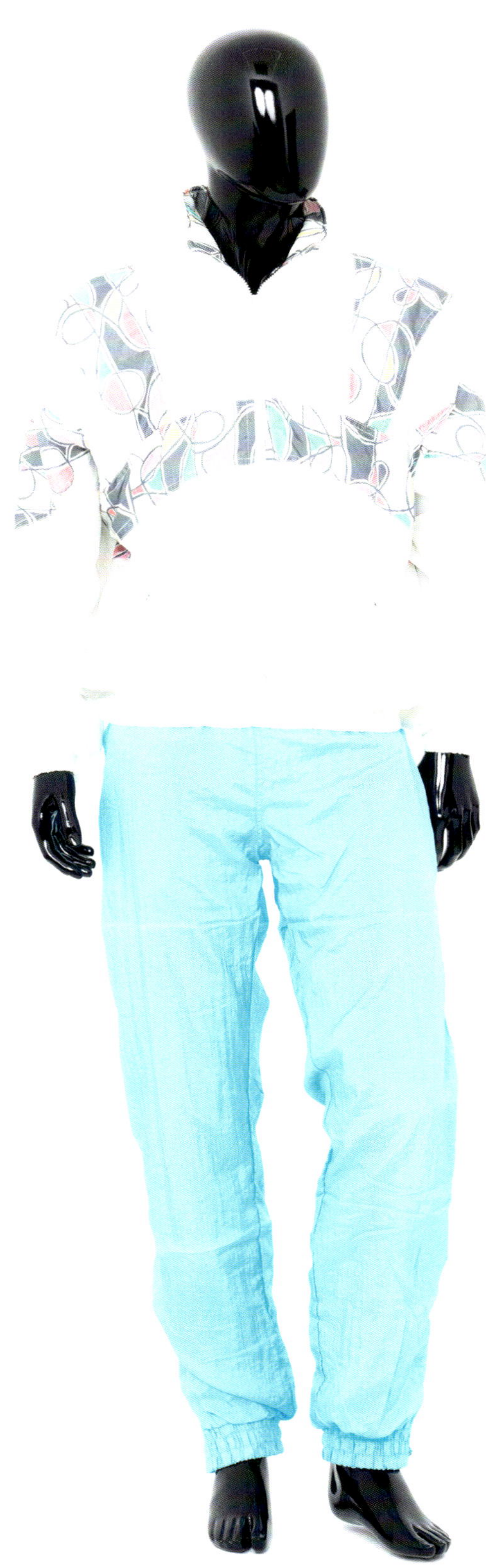

Cat. no. 68

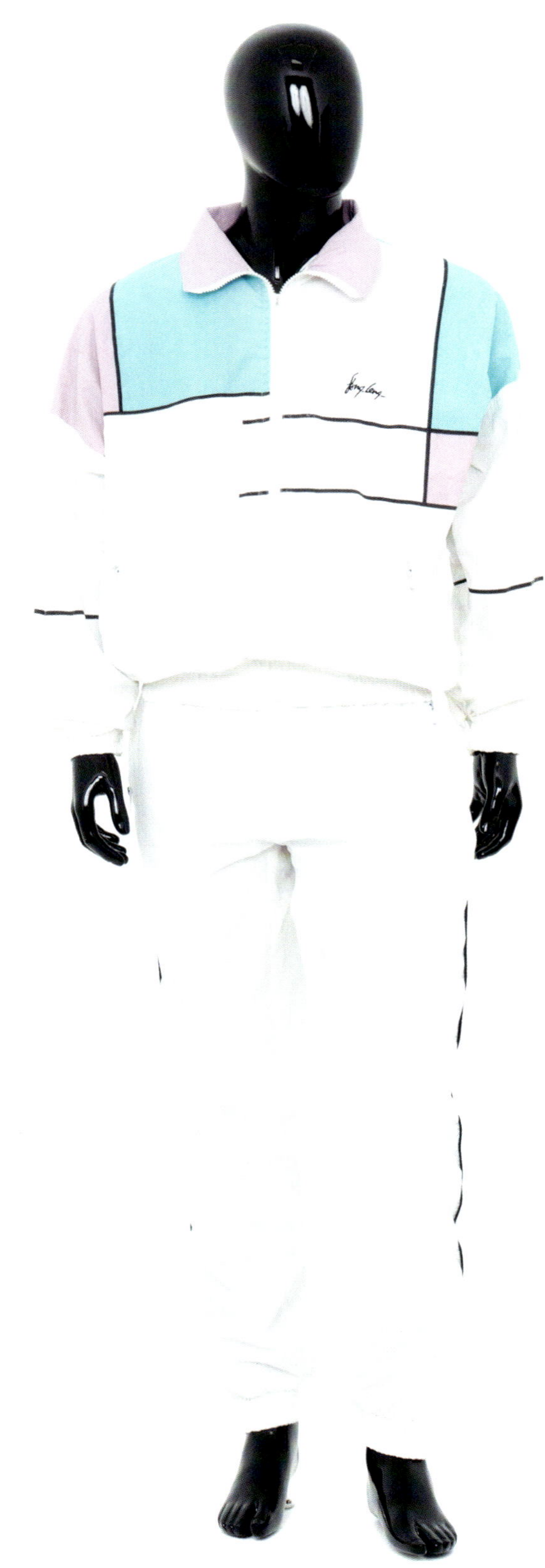

Cat. no. 69

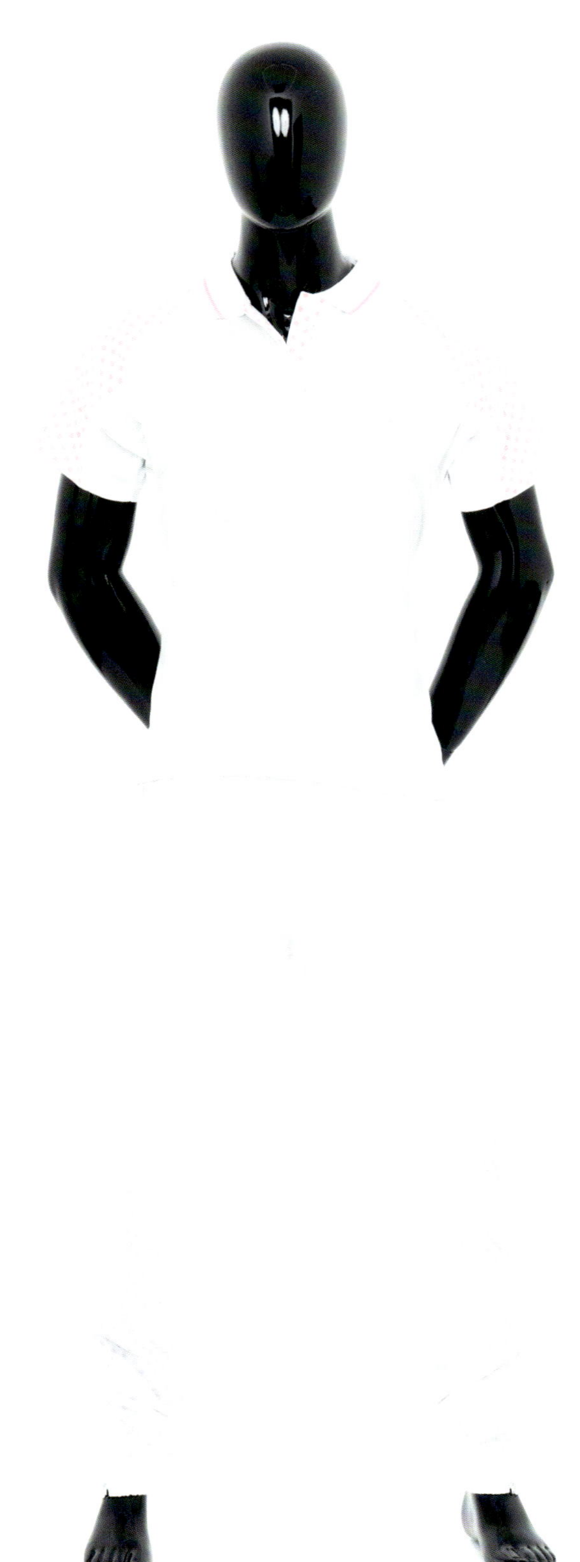

Cat. no. 70

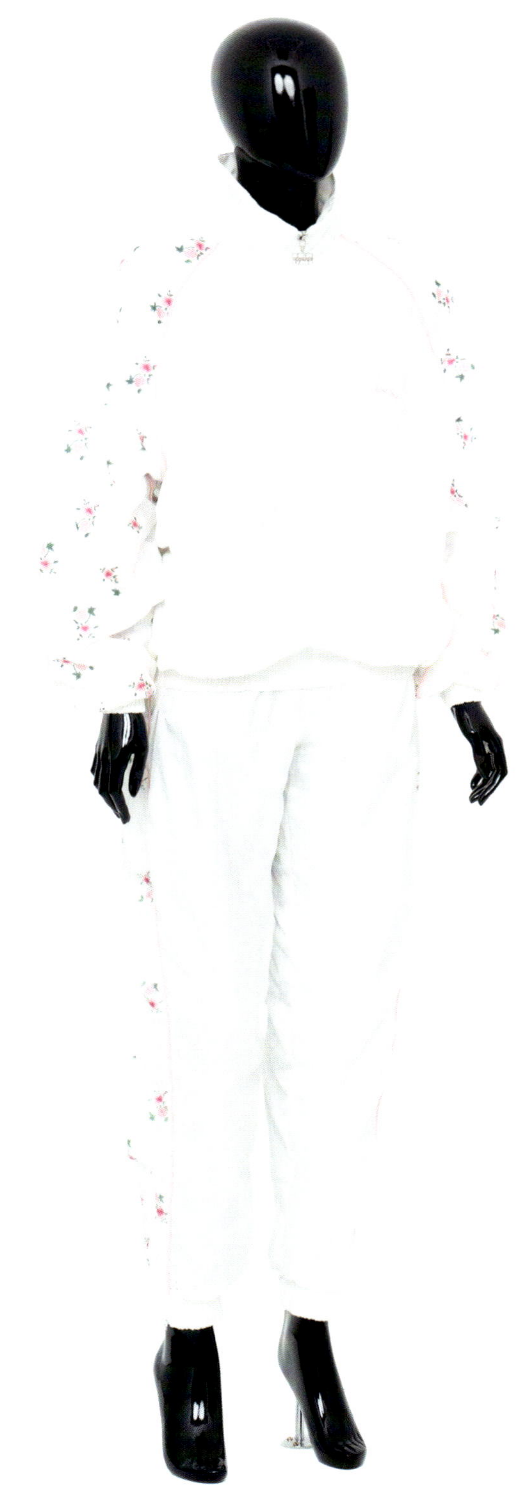

Cat. no. 71

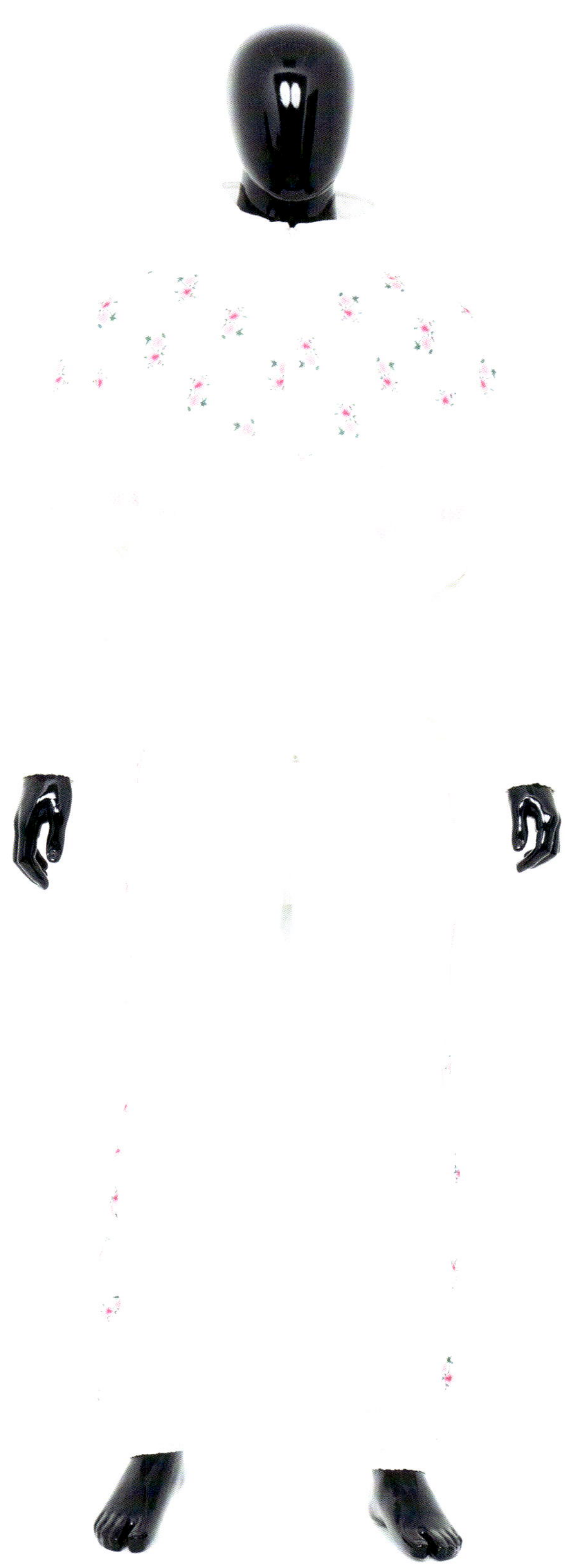

Cat. no. 72

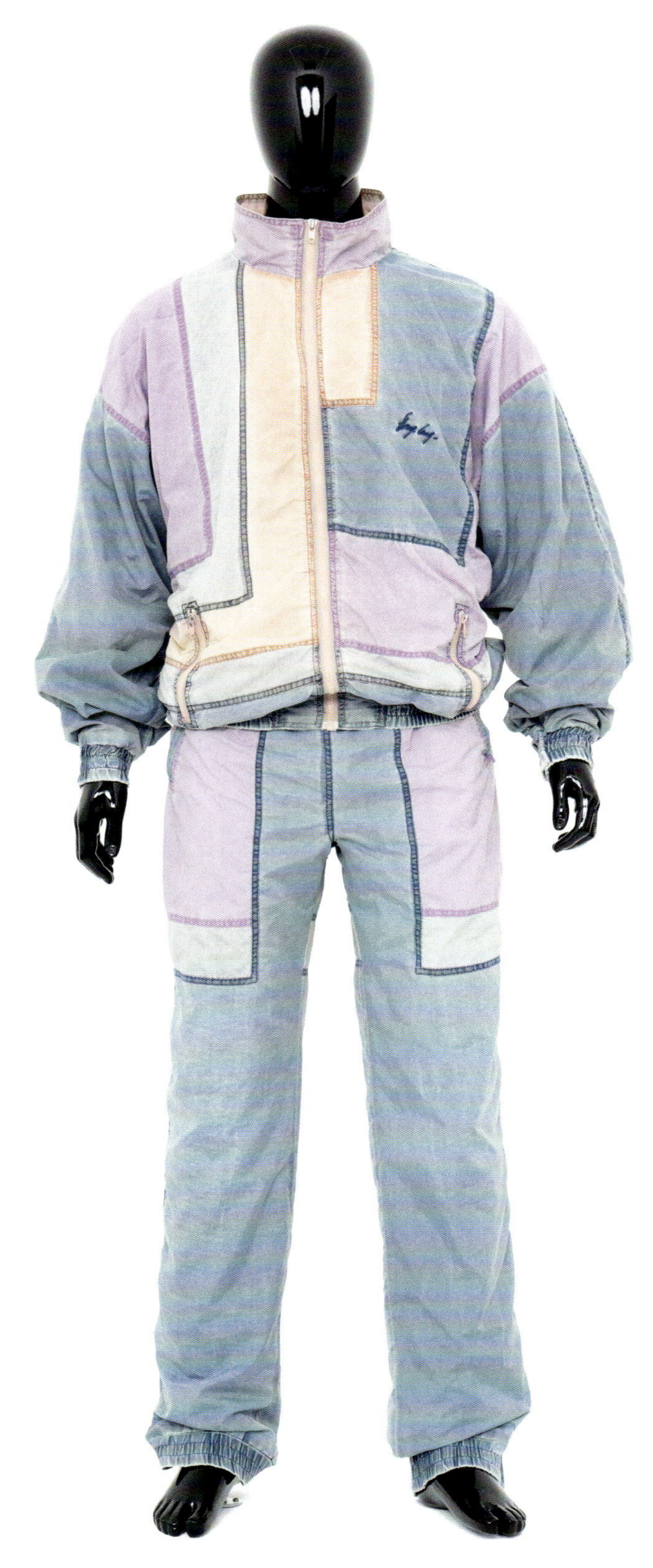

Cat. no. 73

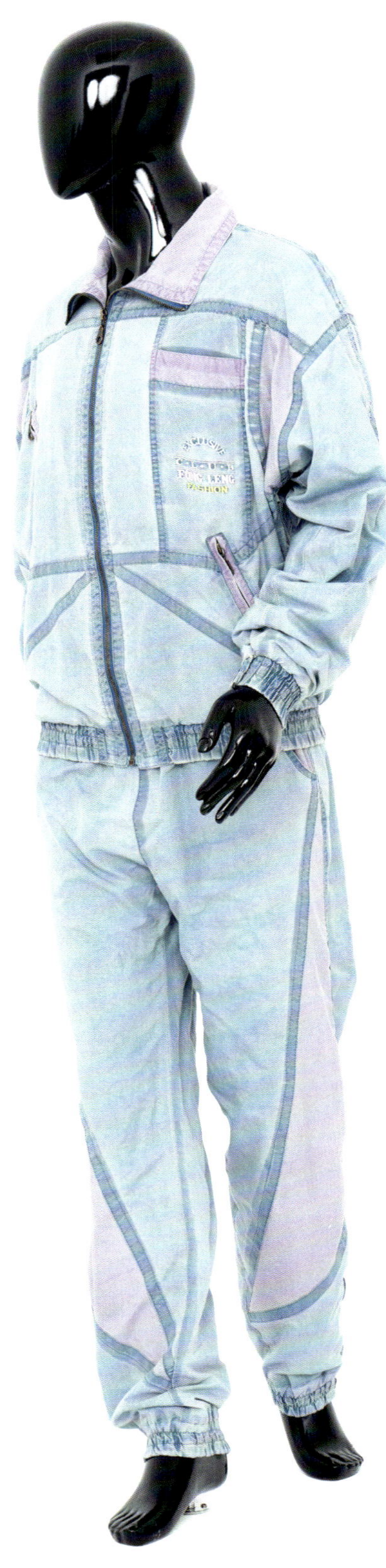

Cat. no. 74

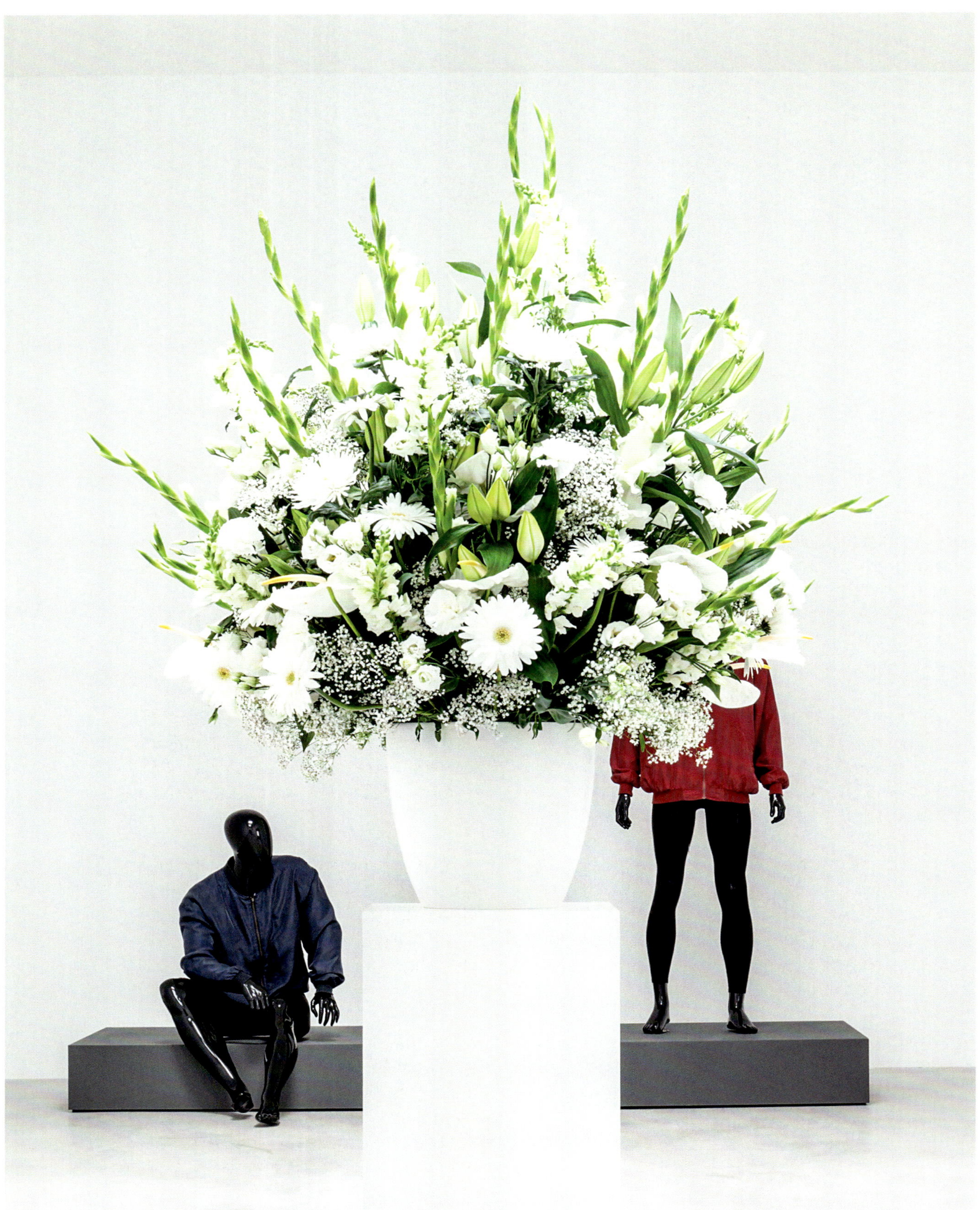

Bouquet IX, 2012

10 different species of flowers, vase, plinth, text (description of the bouquet) and list of flowers (botanic terms)

The work *Bouquet IX, 2012* consists of three parts: a detailed description of the flower arrangement; a complete list of the names of flowers (florist's terms) the arrangement is supposed to consist of, including details of type, color and numbers of flowers; and a certificate of authenticity. The first version of *Bouquet IX, 2012* was executed by Katarzyna Wardecka and Ula Klys for the exhibition *Gript Amok* at Piktogram in Warsaw in September 2012. The realization of this first version can be seen as a collaboration between the artist and Katarzyna Wardecka and Ula Klys.

A detailed description of the bouquet, considering views from all sides, was made by the artist. Based on this description and the list of flowers used for the first version of the bouquet, the work *Bouquet IX, 2012* can be realized in the future.

Description
Bouquet IX, 2012 is created as a spherical shape that is arranged in a cone shaped off-white ceramic vase with an approximate height of 40 cm and (at the top) a diameter of 40 cm. The vase is placed on a white pedestal of 40 × 40 cm and a height of 100 cm. The diameter of the hemisphere measures 100 cm, while the total height of the arrangement, including the vase, adds up to 100 cm.

The overall impression of the arrangement is dense and compact; even though the different flowers vary in size, their even placement in the arrangement creates quite a regular dome-like shape. This order is interrupted only by the long stems of the Gladiola. All different flowers are evenly distributed over the whole, avoiding concentrations of any sort in any area.

The essence of *Bouquet IX, 2012* lies within its color palette—though all flowers used are distinctly different, they are all of the same color: white. Though some flowers may have an incidental leaf on the stem, the color green should not be a dominant factor in the arrangement.

While the Gladiola and snapdragon (Antirrhinum majus) form the longest flowers in the bouquet, the Lilium, Gerbera, Rosa, Carnation, Eustoma and Anthurium form a dense core. The Gypsophila create delicate outbursts that first become apparent on closer inspection.

Willem de Rooij
Bouquet IX, 2012
Installation view *The Impassioned No*
Le Consortium, Dijon (20 June–27 September 2015)

Installation views captions

Page no. 19
Willem de Rooij, *Bouquet IX*, 2012

Page no. 20
Cat. no. 57, 58

Page no. 23
Cat. no. 15, 06, 01, 05, 04, 03

Page no. 25
Cat. no. 55, 02, 69, 16

Page no. 26 (top)
Willem de Rooij, *Bouquet V*, 2010, Collection Haubrok, Berlin
Cat. no. 50, 51, 48, 52, 54, 49, 53

Page no. 26 (bottom)
Peter Fischli & David Weiss, *Concrete Landscape*, 2009, Willem de Rooij, *Silver to Gold*, 2010 and *Bouquet V*, 2010, installation view *LE MONDE COMME VOLONTE ET COMME PAPIER PEINT*, Le Consortium, Dijon 21 April–2 September 2012

Page no. 28
Cat. no. 63, 61, 20, 62

Page no. 29
Cat. no. 45, 46, 47

Page no. 31
Jeroen de Rijke/Willem de Rooij, *Bouquet IV*, 2005, Collection MMK, Museum für Moderne Kunst Frankfurt am Main
Cat. no. 44

Page no. 32, 33
Cat. no. 31, 30, 29, 33, 32, 25, 26, 28, 27, 35

Page no. 35
Cat. no. 35

Page no. 36, 37
Cat. no. 38, 37, 39, 40, 72

Page no. 38
Cat. no. 11, 10, 08, 71

Page no. 39
Jeroen de Rijke/Willem de Rooij, *Bouquet IV*, 2005, Collection MMK, Museum für Moderne Kunst Frankfurt am Main

Catalogue captions

Cat. no. 01
Tracksuit, size S
Shell: 100% trilobal nylon/lining: 65% polyester, 35% cotton
Combination of textiles, applications, embroidered logo, zipper with metal *Fong Leng* puller
Label: with boxing glove
Archive no. TS2

Cat. no. 02
Tracksuit, size XL
Shell: 100% trilobal nylon/lining: 65% polyester, 35% cotton
Combination of textiles, applications, embroidered logo, zipper with metal *Fong Leng* puller
Label: with boxing glove
Archive no. TS5

Cat. no. 03
Tracksuit, size XL
Shell: 100% trilobal nylon/lining: 65% polyester, 35% cotton
Combination of textiles, applications, embroidered logo, zipper with metal *Fong Leng* puller
Label: with boxing glove
Archive no. TS1

Cat. no. 04
Jacket, size S
Shell: 100% trilobal nylon/lining: 65% polyester, 35% cotton
Combination of textiles, applications, embroidered logo, zipper with metal *Fong Leng* puller
Label: with boxing glove
Archive no. TJ10

Cat. no. 05
Jacket, size XL
Shell: 100% trilobal nylon/lining: 65% polyester, 35% cotton
Combination of textiles, applications, prints, zipper with metal *Fong Leng* puller
Label: with boxing glove
Archive no. TJ21

Cat. no. 06
Tracksuit, size M
Shell: 100% trilobal nylon/lining: 65% polyester, 35% cotton
Combination of textiles, applications, embroideries, embroidered logo, zipper with metal *Fong Leng* puller
Label: with boxing glove
Archive no. TS3

Cat. no. 07
Tracksuit, size L
Shell: 100% trilobal nylon/lining: 65% polyester, 35% cotton
Embroideries, embroidered logo, zipper with metal *Fong Leng* puller
Label: with boxing glove
Archive no. TS19

Cat. no. 08
Jacket, size unknown (S)
Material unknown, possibly shell: 100% trilobal nylon/lining: 65% polyester, 35% cotton
Embroideries, embroidered logo, zipper with metal *Fong Leng* puller
Label: with boxing glove
Archive no. TJ3

Cat. no. 09
Polo shirt, size unknown (M)
Material unknown, possibly 50% polyester, 50% cotton
Applications, embroideries, embroidered logo
Label: cut off, possibly with boxing glove
Archive no. SH3

Cat. no. 10
Tracksuit, size unknown (S)
Material unknown, possibly shell: 100% trilobal nylon/lining: 65% polyester, 35% cotton
Combination of textiles, applications, prints, embroidered logo, zipper with metal *Fong Leng* puller
Label: washed out, possibly with tennis racket
Archive no. TS16

Cat. no. 11
Tracksuit, size S
Shell: 100% trilobal nylon/lining: 65% polyester, 35% cotton
Combination of textiles, applications, prints, embroidered logo, zipper with metal *Fong Leng* puller
Label: with tennis racket
Archive no. TS18

Cat. no. 12
Tracksuit, size M
Material unknown, possibly shell: 100% trilobal nylon/lining: 65% polyester, 35% cotton
Combination of textiles, applications, prints, embroidered logo, zipper with metal *Fong Leng* puller
Label: washed out, possibly with tennis racket
Archive no. TS34

Cat. no. 13
Jacket, size unknown
Material unknown
Combination of textiles, applications, prints, printed logo, zipper with metal *Fong Leng* puller
Label: washed out, possibly white
Archive no. TJ28

Cat. no. 14
Tracksuit, size S
Shell and lining: 50% polyester, 50% cotton
Prints, printed logo
Label: white
Archive no. TS35

Cat. no. 15
Jacket, size M
Shell: 100% trilobal nylon/lining: 65% polyester, 35% cotton
Combination of textiles, prints
Label: white
Archive no. TJ26

Cat. no. 16
Tracksuit, size L
Shell and lining: 65% polyester, 35% cotton
Combination of textiles, applications, stitched-on exterior label
Label: white
Archive no. TS4

Cat. no. 17
Jacket, size S
Shell: 100% trilobal nylon/lining and filler: 65% polyester, 35% cotton
Combination of textiles, applications, stitched-on exterior label
Label: white
Archive no. TJ6

Cat. no. 18
Jacket, size L
Shell: 100% newpolyester fiber/lining: 65% polyester, 35% cotton
Combination of textiles, applications, zipper with metal *Fong Leng* puller
Label: black
Archive no. TJ25

Cat. no. 19
Jacket, size L
Shell: 100% newpolyester fiber/lining: 65% polyester, 35% cotton
Applications, embroidered logo, zipper with metal *Fong Leng* puller
Label: black
Archive no. TJ24

Cat. no. 20
Tracksuit, size L
Shell and lining: 65% polyester, 35% cotton
Prints, embroidered logo, zipper with metal *Fong Leng* puller
Label: black
Archive no. TS12

Cat. no. 21
Jacket, size L
Shell: 100% newpolyester fiber/lining: 65% polyester, 35% cotton
Prints, zipper with metal *Fong Leng* puller
Label: black
Archive no. TJ27

Cat. no. 22
Polo shirt, size S
50% Polyester, 50% Cotton
Prints, printed logo
Label: black
Archive no. SH1

Cat. no. 23
Jacket, size L
Shell: 100% newpolyester fiber/lining: 65% polyester, 35% cotton
Combination of textiles, prints, embroidered logo, zipper with metal *Fong Leng* puller
Label: black
Archive no. TJ14

Cat. no. 24
Body warmer, size L
Shell: 65% polyester, 35% cotton/lining: 65% polyester, 35% cotton
Combination of textiles, prints, embroidered logo, zipper with metal *Fong Leng* puller
Label: black
Archive no. DTS1

Cat. no. 25
3-part tracksuit (jacket, body warmer, pants), size S
Shell and lining: 65% polyester, 35% cotton
Combination of textiles, prints, embroidered logo, zipper with metal *Fong Leng* puller
Label: black
Archive no. DTS3

Cat. no. 26
3-part tracksuit (jacket, body warmer, pants), size L, XL
Shell and lining: 65% polyester, 35% cotton
Combination of textiles, prints, embroidered logo, zipper with metal *Fong Leng* puller
Label: black
Archive no. DTS1

Cat. no. 27
3-part tracksuit (jacket, body warmer, pants), size XL
Shell and lining: 65% polyester, 35% cotton
Combination of textiles, prints, embroidered logo, zipper with metal *Fong Leng* puller
Label: black
Archive no. DTS2

Cat. no. 28
Tracksuit, size M
Shell and lining: 65% polyester, 35% cotton
Combination of textiles, prints, embroidered logo, zipper with metal *Fong Leng* puller
Label: black
Archive no. TS10

Cat. no. 29
Jacket, size L
Shell and lining: 65% polyester, 35% cotton
Combination of textiles, prints, embroidered logo, zipper with metal *Fong Leng* puller
Label: black
Archive no. TJ12

Cat. no. 30
Jacket, size S
Shell and lining: 50% polyester, 50% cotton
Combination of textiles, prints, embroidered logo
Label: black
Archive no. TJ23

Cat. no. 31
Body warmer, size S
Shell and lining: 50% polyester, 50% cotton
Combination of textiles, prints, embroidered logo, zipper with metal *Fong Leng* puller
Label: black
Archive no. B1

Cat. no. 32
Tracksuit, size XL
Shell and lining: 65% polyester, 35% cotton
Combination of textiles, prints, embroidered logo, zipper with metal *Fong Leng* puller
Label: black
Archive no. TS30

Cat. no. 33
Tracksuit, size XL
Shell and lining: 65% polyester, 35% cotton
Combination of textiles, prints, embroidered logo, zipper with metal *Fong Leng* puller
Label: black
Archive no. TS37

Cat. no. 34
Tracksuit, size L
Shell and lining: 65% polyester, 35% cotton
Combination of textiles, prints, zipper with metal *Fong Leng* puller
Label: black
Archive no. TS31

Cat. no. 35
3-part tracksuit (jacket, t-shirt, pants), size L
Jacket and pants
Shell and lining: 65% polyester, 35% cotton
T-Shirt
60% cotton, 40% polyester
Combination of textiles, prints, embroidered logo, zipper with metal *Fong Leng* puller
Label: black
Archive no. DTS4

Cat. no. 36
3-part tracksuit (jacket, body warmer, pants), size M
Shell and lining: 50% polyester, 50% cotton
Combination of textiles, prints, embroidered logo, zipper with metal *Fong Leng* puller
Label: black
Archive no. DTS5

Cat. no. 37
Tracksuit, size M
Shell: 100% newpolyester nylon/lining: 65% polyester, 35% cotton
Combination of textiles, prints, embroidered logo, zipper with metal *Fong Leng* puller

Label: black
Archive no. TS7

Cat. no. 38
Tracksuit, size XL
Shell: 100% newpolyester nylon/lining: 65% polyester, 35% cotton
Combination of textiles, prints, embroidered logo, zipper with metal *Fong Leng* puller
Label: black
Archive no. TS6

Cat. no. 39
Tracksuit, size S
Shell: 100% newpolyester nylon/lining: 65% polyester, 35% cotton
Combination of textiles, prints, embroidered logo, zipper with metal *Fong Leng* puller
Label: black
Archive no. TS9

Cat. no. 40
Tracksuit, size L
Shell: 100% newpolyester nylon/lining: 65% polyester, 35% cotton
Combination of textiles, prints, embroidered logo, zipper with metal *Fong Leng* puller
Label: black
Archive no. TS8

Cat. no. 41
Jacket, size XL
Shell: 100% newpolyester fiber/lining: 65% polyester, 35% cotton
Embroideries, embroidered logo, zipper with metal *Fong Leng* puller
Label: black
Archive no. TJ22

Cat. no. 42
Jacket, size L
Shell: 100% newpolyester fiber/lining: 65% polyester, 35% cotton
Embroideries, embroidered logo, zipper with metal *Fong Leng* puller
Label: black
Archive no. TJ8

Cat. no. 43
Tracksuit, size L
Shell: 100% newpolyester fiber/lining: 65% polyester, 35% cotton
Combination of textiles, prints, embroideries, embroidered logo, zipper with metal *Fong Leng* puller
Label: black
Archive no. TS15

Cat. no. 44
Jacket, size XL
Shell: 65% polyester, 35% nylon/lining and filler: 100% polyester
Collar adorned with faux fur
Label: black
Archive no. J1

Cat. no. 45
Jacket, size L
Shell: 100 % nylon/lining: 100 % nylon/ filler: 100 % polyester
Prints, collar adorned with faux fur, zipper with metal *Fong Leng* puller
Label: Exclusive Club black
Archive no. J5

Cat. no. 46
Jacket, size unknown (M)
Shell: 100 % nylon/lining: 100 % nylon/ filler: 100 % polyester
Prints, zipper with metal *Fong Leng* puller (broken)
Label: Exclusive Club black
Archive no. J6

Cat. no. 47
Jacket, size L
Shell: 100 % nylon/lining: 100 % nylon/ filler: 100 % polyester
Prints, collar adorned with faux fur
Label: Exclusive Club black
Archive no. J7

Cat. no. 48
Fleece jacket, size X
Shell: 100 % polyester/lining: 100 % nylon
Prints, zipper with metal *Fong Leng* puller
Label: Exclusive Club black
Archive no. T1

Cat. no. 49
Fleece pullover, size unknown (M)
Shell: 100% polyester
Prints, embroidered logo, zipper with metal *Fong Leng* puller
Label: Exclusive Club black
Archive no. T18

Cat. no. 50
Fleece jacket, size M
Shell: 100% polyester/lining: 100% nylon
Prints, embroidered logo
Label: Exclusive Club black
Archive no. T4

Cat. no. 51
Fleece jacket, size M
Shell: 100% polyester, 65% polyester, 35% cotton/lining: 100% nylon/filler: 100% polyester
Combination of textiles, prints
Label: Exclusive Club black
Archive no. T5

Cat. no. 52
Fleece jacket, size L
Shell: 100% polyester/lining: 100% nylon
Prints, embroidered logo
Label: Exclusive Club black
Archive no. T2

Cat. no. 53
Fleece pullover, size L
Shell: 100% polyester
Prints, embroidered logo
Label: Exclusive Club black
Archive no. T3

Cat. no. 54
Fleece jacket, size M
Shell: 100% polyester/lining: 100% nylon
Prints, zipper with metal *Fong Leng* puller
Label: Exclusive Club 'Total Controll Sportswear and Outdoor Garment'
Archive no. T19

Cat. no. 55
Fleece pullover, size M
Shell: 100% polyester/lining: 100% nylon
Combination of textiles, applications, embroidered logo
Label: Exclusive Club black
Archive no. T6

Cat. no. 56
Jumper, size L
Shell and lining: 100% nylon
Embroidered label (*American Skiing In*), zipper with metal *Fong Leng* puller
Label: Exclusive Club black
Archive no. J3

Cat. no. 57
Jacket, size unknown (XXL)
Shell: 100% silk/lining: 100% polyamide
Label: Exclusive Club black
Archive no. TJ18

Cat. no. 58
Jacket, size XXL
Shell: 100% silk/lining: 100% polyamide
Label: Exclusive Club black
Archive no. TJ20

Cat. no. 59
Tracksuit, size XXL
Shell: 65% polyester, 35% viscose/ lining: 50% polyester, 50% cotton
Prints, embroidered logo
Label: Exclusive Club black
Archive no. TS36

Cat. no. 60
Jacket, size XL
Shell and lining: 65% polyester,

35% cotton
Prints, embroidered logo
Label: Exclusive Club black
Archive no. TJ11

Cat. no. 61
Jacket, size L
Shell and lining: 65% polyester, 35% cotton
Prints, embroidered logo
Label: Exclusive Club black
Archive no. TJ5

Cat. no. 62
Jacket, size L
Shell and lining: 65% polyester, 35% cotton
Prints, embroidered logo, zipper with metal *Fong Leng* puller
Label: Exclusive Club black
Archive no. TJ30

Cat. no. 63
Jacket, size M
Shell and lining: 65% polyester, 35% cotton
Prints, embroidered label, zipper with metal *Fong Leng* puller
Label: *Fong Leng voor Vomar*—Exclusive Club black
Archive no. TJ13

Cat. no. 64
Tracksuit, size S
Shell and lining: 65% polyester, 35% cotton
Prints, embroidered logo, zipper with metal *Fong Leng* puller
Label: Exclusive Club black
Archive no. TS28

Cat. no. 65
Jacket, size L
Shell: 100% trilobal nylon/lining: 65% polyester, 35% cotton
Combination of textiles, prints, zipper with metal *Fong Leng* puller
Label: Exclusive Club black
Archive no. TJ9

Cat. no. 66
Tracksuit, size L
Shell: 100% trilobal nylon/lining: 65% polyester, 35% cotton
Combination of textiles, prints, embroidered logo
Label: Exclusive Club black
Archive no. TS24

Cat. no. 67
Tracksuit, size XL
Shell: 100 % trilobal nylon/lining: 65% polyester, 35 % cotton
Combination of textiles, prints, zipper with metal *Fong Leng* puller
Label: Exclusive Club black
Archive no. TS20

Cat. no. 68
Tracksuit, size L
Shell: 100% trilobal nylon/lining: 65% polyester, 35% cotton
Combination of textiles, prints
Label: Exclusive Club black
Archive no. TS27

Cat. no. 69
Tracksuit, size M
Shell: 65% cotton, 35% polyester/lining: 35% polyester, 65% cotton
Combination of textiles, prints, embroidered logo
Label: Exclusive Club black
Archive no. TS29

Cat. no. 70
2-part outfit, size XL, L
Pants, size XL
Shell: 65% cotton, 35% polyester/lining: 65% polyester, 35% cotton
Label: Exclusive Club black
Polo shirt, size L
100% Cotton
Label: Exclusive Club white
Combination of textiles, prints, embroidered logo
Archive no. TB5, SH2

Cat. no. 71
Tracksuit, size S
Shell: 100% trilobal nylon/lining: 65% polyester, 35% cotton
Combination of textiles, prints, applications, embroidered logo, zipper with metal *Fong Leng* puller
Label: Exclusive Club black
Archive no. TS17

Cat. no. 72
Tracksuit, size M
Shell: 100% trilobal nylon/lining: 65% polyester, 35% cotton
Combination of textiles, prints, applications, embroidered logo
Label: Exclusive Club black
Archive no. TS38

Cat. no. 73
Tracksuit, size XXL
Shell: 100% taslan nylon/lining: 65% polyester, 35% cotton
Combination of textiles, embroidered logo
Label: Exclusive Club white
Archive no. TS33

Cat. no. 74
Tracksuit, size L
Shell: 100% taslan nylon/lining: 65% polyester, 35% cotton
Combination of textiles, embroidered logo
Label: Exclusive Club white
Archive no. TS13

Details

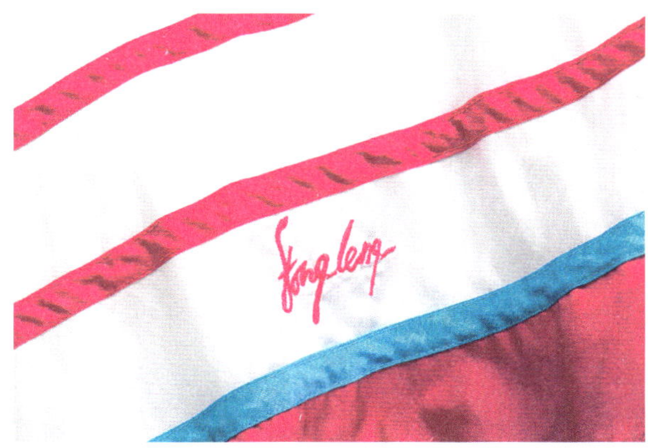

Detail no. I
Detail of Archive no. TS5, Cat. no. 02

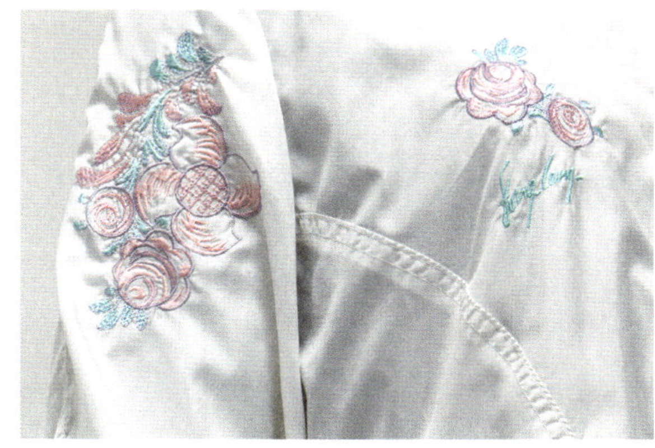

Detail no. II
Detail of Archive no. TJ3, Cat. no. 08

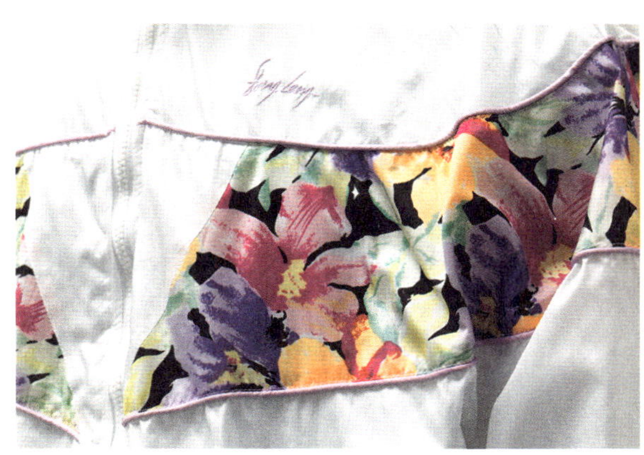

Detail no. III
Detail of Archive no. TS18, Cat. no. 11

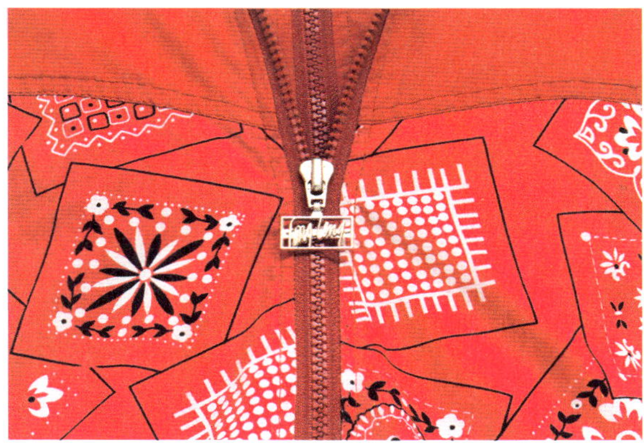

Detail no. IV
Detail of Archive no. DTS1, Cat. no. 26

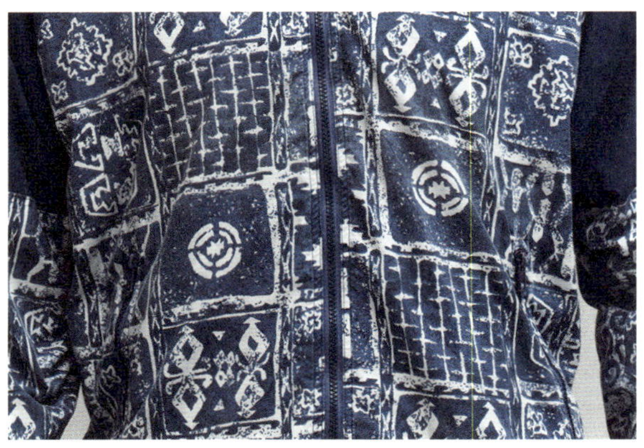

Detail no. V
Detail of Archive no. TJ23, Cat. no. 30

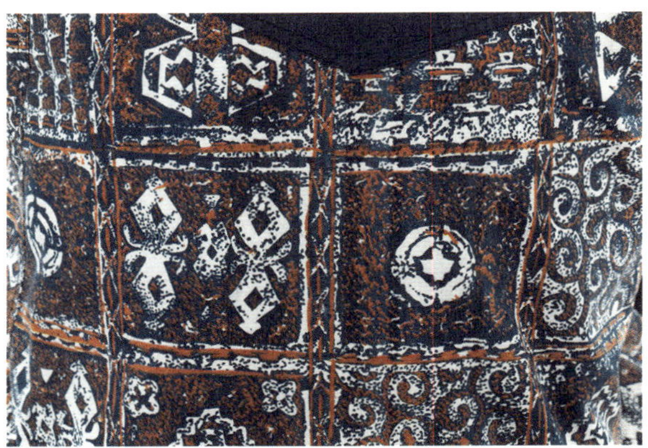

Detail no. VI
Detail of Archive no. B1, Cat. no. 31

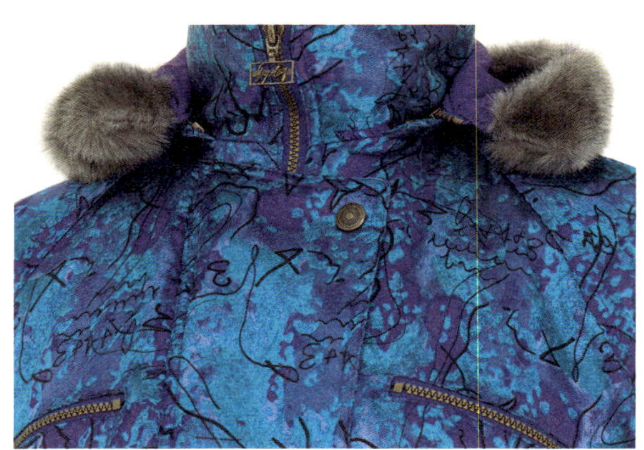

Detail no. VII
Detail of Archive no. J5, Cat. no. 45

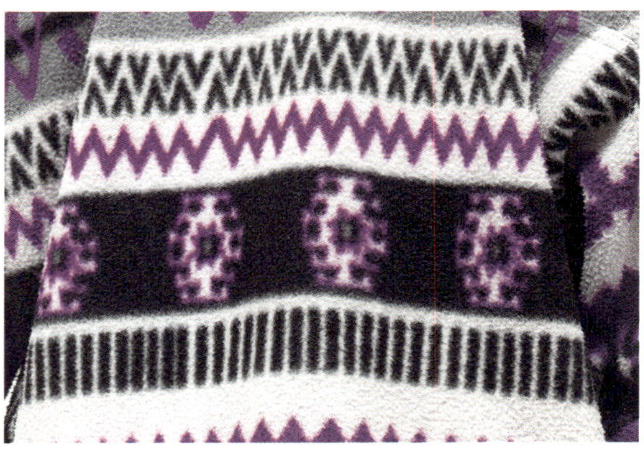

Detail no. VIII
Detail of Archive no. T4, Cat. no. 50

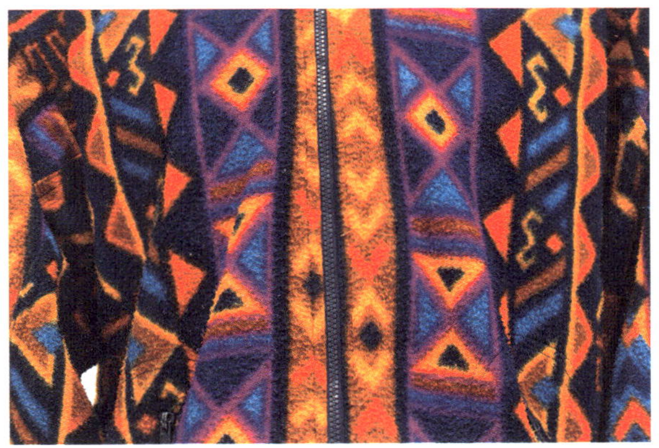

Detail no. IX
Detail of Archive no. T2, Cat. no. 52

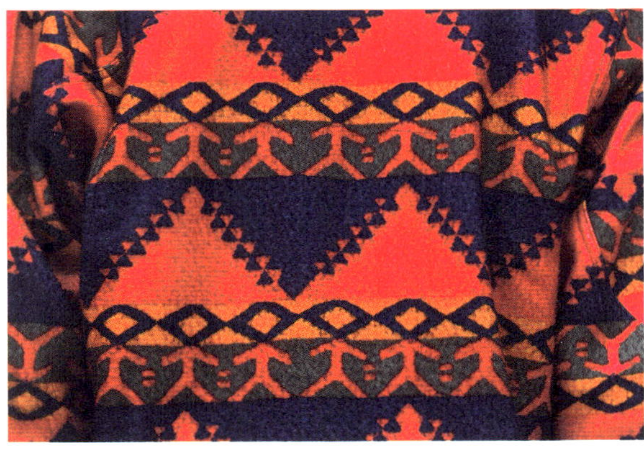

Detail no. X
Detail of Archive no. T19 (shell), Cat. no. 54

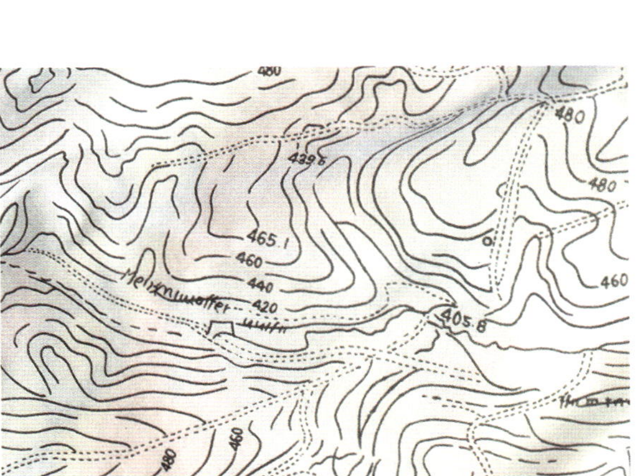

Detail no. XI
Detail of Archive no. T19 (lining), Cat. no. 54

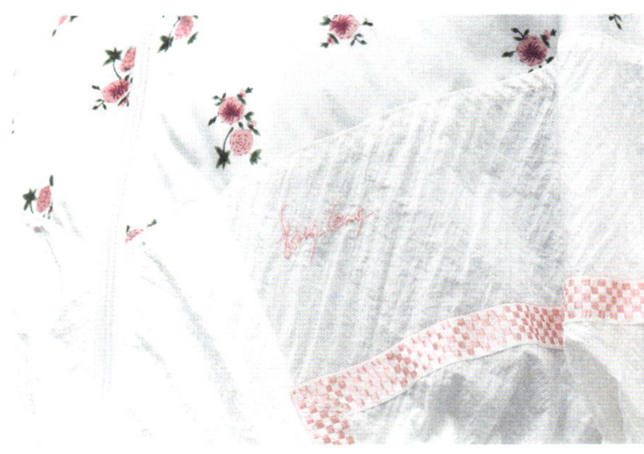

Detail no. XII
Detail of Archive no. TS38, Cat. no. 72

Labels

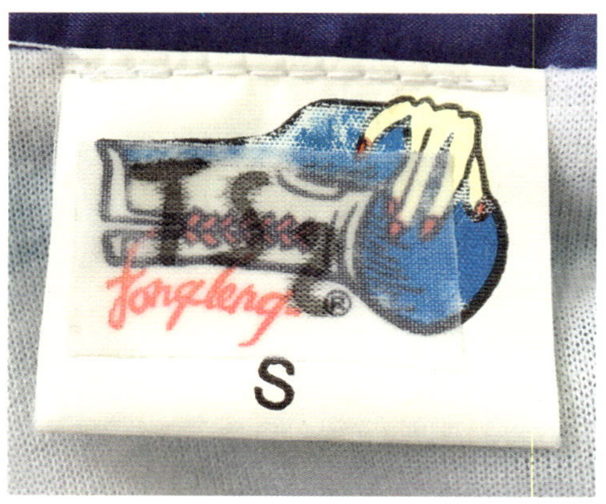

Label no. I
Fong Leng label with boxing glove
Detail of Archive no. TS2, Cat. no. 01

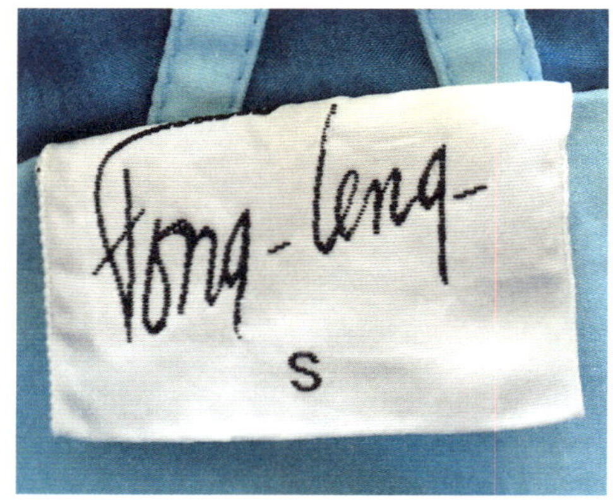

Label no. II
Fong Leng white label
Detail of Archive no. TJ6, Cat. no. 17

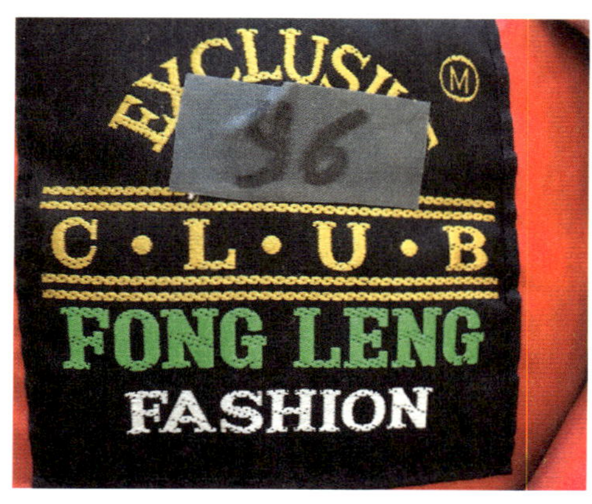

Label no. III
Fong Leng Exclusive Club black label
Detail of Archive no. J6, Cat. no. 46

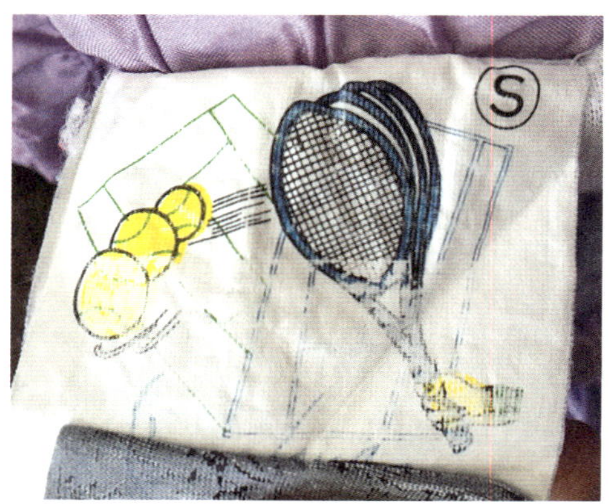

Label no. IV
Fong Leng label with tennis racket
Detail of Archive no. TS18, Cat. no. 11

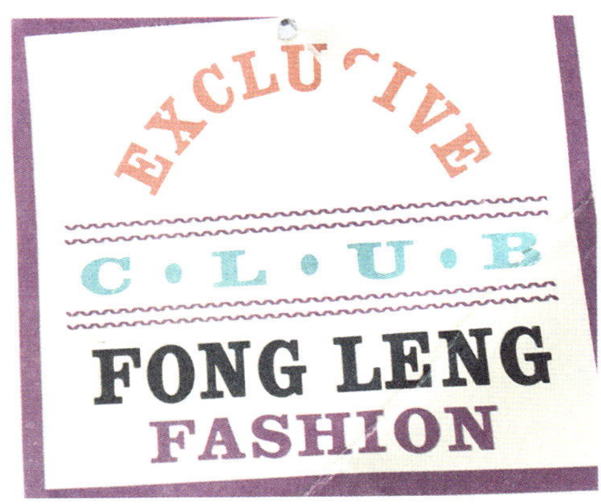

Label no. V
Fong Leng Exclusive Club tag

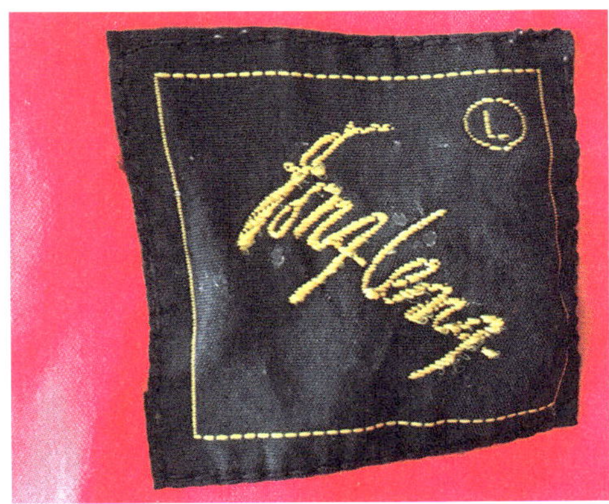

Label no. VI
Fong Leng black label
Detail of Archive no. DTS1, Cat. no. 26

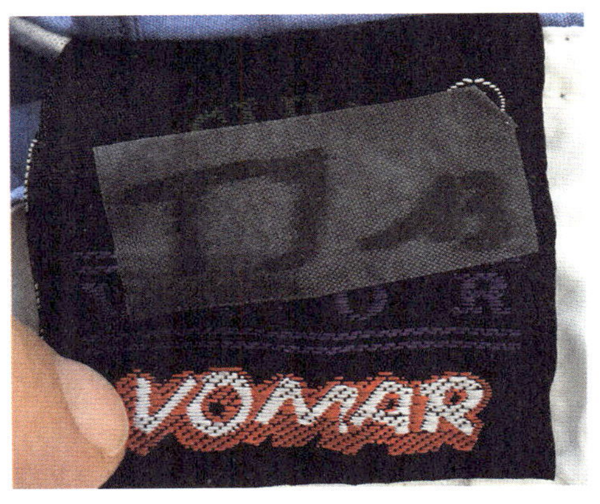

Label no. VII
Fong Leng voor Vomar
Exclusive Club black label
Detail of Archive no. TJ13, Cat. no. 63

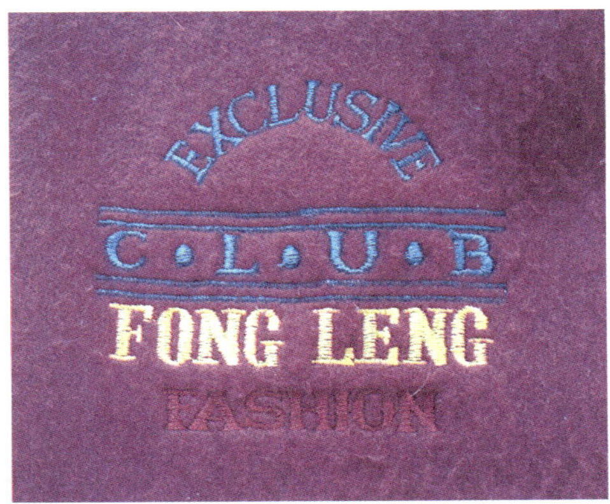

Label no. VIII
Fong Leng Exclusive Club embroidered logo
Detail of Archive no. T6, Cat. no. 55

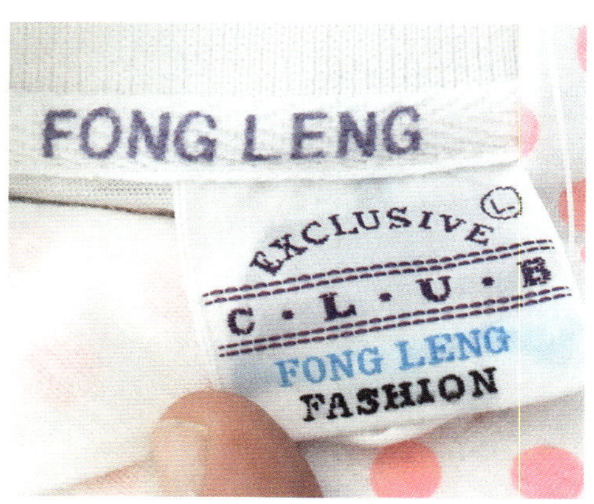

Label no. IX
Fong Leng white label
Detail of Archive no. TB5, Cat. no. 70

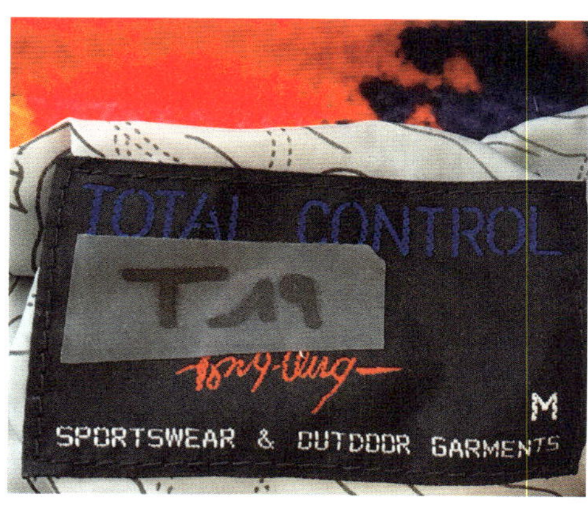

Label no. X
Fong Leng Exclusive Club black label
'Total Control'
Detail of Archive no. T19, Cat. no. 54

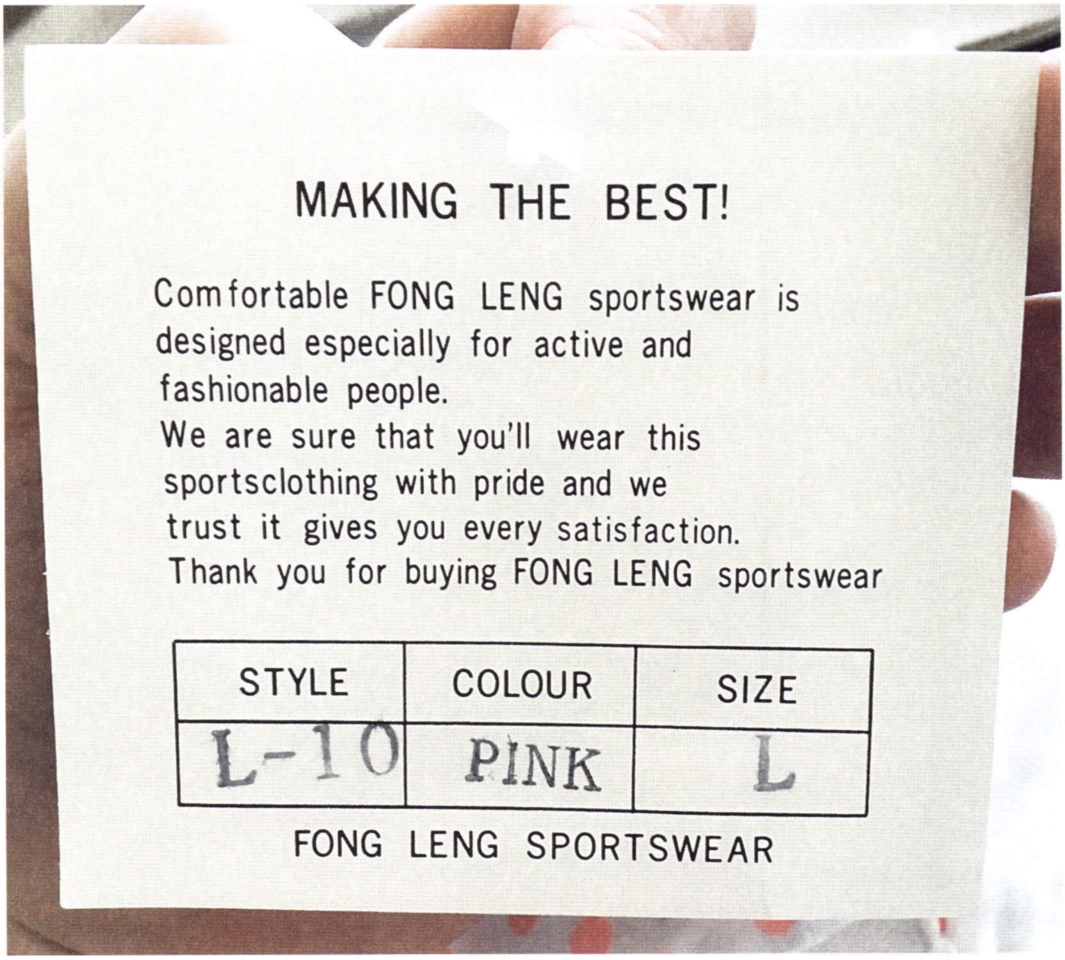

Label no. XI
Fong Leng guarantee tag

The artist thanks:
Daniel Buchholz
Chantal Crousel
Keren Cytter
Fong Leng
Isa Genzken
Bart van der Heide
Gianfranco Maraniello
Christopher Müller
Niklas Svennung
Andrea Viliani
Vincent Vulsma

Colophon

This book is published on the occasion of solo exhibitions of Willem de Rooij: The Impassioned No, Le Consortium, Dijon (20 June–27 September 2015) and Entitled, MMK Museum für Moderne Kunst Frankfurt am Main (14 October 2016–8 January 2017).

Published by:
Le Consortium, Dijon
MMK Museum für Moderne Kunst Frankfurt am Main
Galerie Buchholz, Cologne/Berlin
Friedrich Petzel Gallery, New York
Galerie Chantal Crousel, Paris
Regen Projects, Los Angeles

Koenig Books, London Ltd
Kensington Gardens
At the Serpentine Gallery
London W2 3XA
www.koenigbooks.co.uk

Bibliographic information published by the Deutsche Nationalbibliothek

The Deutsche Nationalbibliothek lists this publication in the Deutsche Nationalbibliografie; detailed bibliographic data are available in the Internet at http://dnb.d-nb.de.

Printed in Germany

Editor:
Willem de Rooij, Susanne Gaensheimer

Production Management:
Mailena Mallach

Design:
Markus Weisbeck, Victor Kassis, Surface Gesellschaft für Gestaltung Frankfurt am Main/Berlin

Print:
NINO Druck GmbH, Neustadt/Wstr.

Lithography:
Der Ripperger Medienproduktion GmbH

Archive Fong Leng:
Jasmijn Visser

Image Credits:
André Morin, pp. 19–39, 135–137
Pierre Even, Cat. no. 01–74, p. 128
Diane Arques, p. 26 (bottom)
Willem de Rooij, pp. 138–141

Essays:
Stéphanie Moisdon, Philipp Ekardt, Manfred Hermes

Translation:
Jacob Bromberg

Copy editing:
Willem de Rooij

Proof reading:
Jennifer Heber-Brown

Willem de Rooij Studio:
Mailena Mallach, Jasmijn Visser

Le Consortium
37 rue de Longvic
21000 Dijon
France
www.leconsortium.fr

Director/Co-Director: Xavier Douroux, Seungduk Kim, Franck Gautherot, Stéphanie Moisdon, Anne Pontégnie, Éric Troncy
Curator: Stéphanie Moisdon

MMK Museum für Moderne Kunst
Frankfurt am Main
Domstraße 10
60311 Frankfurt am Main
Germany
T +49 69 212 304 47
F +49 69 212 378 82
www.mmk-frankfurt.de

Director: Susanne Gaensheimer
Curator: Klaus Görner

Distribution:
Germany & Europe
Buchhandlung Walther König
Ehrenstr. 4, 50672 Köln
Tel. +49 (0) 221 20 59 6 53
Fax +49 (0) 221 20 59 6 60
verlag@buchhandlung-walther-koenig.de

UK & Ireland
Cornerhouse Publications
HOME
2 Tony Wilson Place
UK–Manchester M15 4FN
Fon +44 (0) 161 212 34 66
Fax: +44 (0) 175 220 23 30
publications@cornerhouse.org

Outside Europe
D.A.P./Distributed Art Publishers, Inc.
155 6th Avenue, 2nd Floor
USA-New York, NY 10013
Fon +1 (0) 212 627 1999
Fax +1 (0) 212 627 9484
eleshowitz@dapinc.com

ISBN 978-3-86335-724-5

Le Consortium
·centre d'art·

MMK MUSEUM FÜR MODERNE KUNST FRANKFURT AM MAIN

Koenig Books, London

Galerie Buchholz

Galerie
Chantal Crousel

Petzel

REGEN PROJECTS